Margaret Laird

RELIGIOUS AND MORAL EDUCATION PRESS

Religious and Moral Education Press
A division of SCM-Canterbury Press Ltd
A wholly owned subsidiary of Hymns Ancient & Modern Ltd
St Mary's Works, St Mary's Plain
Norwich, Norfolk NR3 3BH

First published 2001

ISBN 1 85175 255 2

The author and publisher thank the owners or controllers of copyright for permission to use the copyright material listed below. Every effort has been made to contact copyright owners and the author and publisher apologize to any whose rights have inadvertently not been acknowledged.

The poem 'Apologue on the Parable of the Wedding Garment', by Charles Williams, is reproduced by permission of David Higham Associates.

The prayer 'I Want to Be Somebody' is reproduced by permission from *Meet Christ and Live*, by Abbé Michel Quoist, published by Gill & Macmillan.

Extracts from *The Alternative Service Book 1980* are copyright © The Archbishops' Council and are reproduced by permission.

'Prayer for the Third Millennium', by Anna Crompton, is reproduced by permission of The Open Churches Trust.

The painting 'The Ringers of Launcells', by Frederick Smallfield, is © the Royal Institution of Cornwall and is reproduced by permission.

Designed and typeset by Topics – The Creative Partnership, Exeter
Illustrations by Jane Taylor
Printed in Great Britain by Brightsea Press, Exeter, for SCM-Canterbury Press Ltd, Norwich

A Foreword by the Archbishop of York, Dr David Hope

It was F. Scott Fitzgerald who said that, 'an author ought to write for the young people of his own generation, the critics of the next and the school masters of ever afterwards.' Margaret Laird has fulfilled these demanding criteria of authorship in a quite remarkable way. She has, indeed, written for the young people of today. Not *at* them, or *down to* them, but *for* them. She engages with young minds in their quest for meaning and purpose; she excites their natural curiosity and a sense of wonder; and she manages to do it all in a way which respects both their intelligence and their integrity.

But then each of these 'assemblies' has been forged in a very practical context of Margaret Laird's own daily experience over a long number of years. Here is a book which is every bit as much for the teachers as for the taught. Teachers who, in the over-heated educational climate of today, are under greater pressures than their profession has ever known: teachers who may feel that they simply do not have either the time, the resources or even the confidence to develop their own material. Or, perhaps, teachers who may entertain some reservations about the wisdom or propriety of such assemblies.

The scope of the material is considerable as it is searching, ranging as it does from questions about being and existence, and daring to enquire into life beyond this life, as well as a comprehensive journey through the Christian year.

The Christian message is set out clearly and boldly, in a wholly ecumenical context, yet in a way which always ensures a proper respect and honour towards those of other faiths.

I am enormously encouraged by the depth and richness of this resource book, and I commend it - not only to those teachers in secondary schools for whom it has been written - but for clergy and others who are engaged in formative work with young people. I believe that all will find it hugely rewarding as much for themselves as for others.

†David Ebor:

Contents

Acknowledgements

The seeds for these assemblies were sown many years ago at Truro High School, and it is to Miss Gladys Engledow, the Headmistress when I was there, that I am greatly indebted. Her daily assemblies provided the framework in which the life of the school was firmly set, and were the means by which her own Christian conviction and sensible approach to practical living influenced the lives of her pupils. I am well aware that school life is very different these days, but this is no excuse for not expressing my gratitude to someone who long ago demonstrated to me the beneficial effect of a regular daily assembly.

To return to the present, I must express my thanks to Mrs Mary Mears of RMEP for her invaluable support. Contact with the world of publishing was a new experience for me and I am especially grateful for her guidance and her professionalism.

I am also deeply indebted to Bishop Alec Graham, formerly Bishop of Newcastle and sometime Chairman of the Church of England Doctrine Commission. He graciously agreed to read my scripts to ensure that I did not fall into theological error, but being the meticulous scholar that he is, he also picked up other minor points which needed to be corrected or rephrased. I must therefore thank him for his much valued and constructive comments and the occasional gentle rebuke!

To Mr Patrick Locke, who discussed the project with me in its early stages, I am grateful, and also to Mrs Elizabeth Marsh, who directed me to RMEP as a publishing house which would be sympathetic to my objectives. I am also greatly indebted to the distinguished Cornish painter John Miller, who generously provided the cover illustration.

Without the practical secretarial help of Barbara Brooks and more recently Marion Davies, progress would have been impossible and I thank them both for their conscientiousness, genuine interest and immaculately typed pages.

My acknowledgements would not be complete without expressing how much I owe to my former pupils, especially those of the Dame Alice Harpur School, whose enquiring minds and enthusiastic responses inspired so many of these assemblies, and to Brother Michael SSF, who encouraged me to think in terms of publication. Having gained so much benefit from his wise advice in the past, I knew that any suggestion he made had to be taken seriously.

The greatest debt of all, however, I owe to my husband John and our sons Andrew and Stephen, for their good-humoured endurance. It was from those frantically busy years, when the four of us were totally immersed in school life as teachers or pupils, that the ideas emerged, were subjected to severe and often amusing family criticism, and then delivered more or less in their present form as assembly material.

Margaret Laird

Introduction

This book is designed to provide a resource for those who conduct assemblies for older secondary students in church comprehensive schools or in independent schools with a Christian foundation, of which there are still many. It is my hope, however, that the themes will also prove helpful to teachers in any school or college with students of that age group.

This collection of talks results from my experience of teaching and of conducting assemblies in a wide range of schools, most recently in an area with a high proportion of ethnic minority groups, who were well represented in the classrooms. Many of the talks were inspired by questions asked by students themselves or were the result of discussions in Religious Education lessons. So often, these questions were on subjects which have exercised the minds of philosophers and theologians from ancient times to the present day. Consequently, the units aim to encourage a thoughtful approach to religion, to help students gain some understanding of theological and philosophical concepts and to show how a spiritual dimension to life can prove beneficial, not only to the individual but to society as a whole.

Secondly, many of the themes attempt to demonstrate how religion and culture are intrinsically linked. They draw upon works of literature and art, both secular and religious, and provide information about influential, unusual and interesting men and women, past and present.

My third objective is to provide some understanding of the pattern of the Christian year and the importance of the great Church festivals, to encourage an atmosphere of worship and to evoke an intelligent response to material which appeals to enquiring minds without in any way playing upon the emotions.

The talks are printed more or less in the form in which they were delivered, which means that some of them are introduced in the first person singular. No attempt has been made to change this personal approach because whatever adaptations one might have made, teachers will inevitably choose to present the material in a style and in a way which is distinctively their own.

In the arrangement of this book, everything possible has been done to save teachers valuable time. In most cases, both a 'thought' and a 'prayer' have been attached to the talks in order to give flexibility. The 'thought', for example, could provide a final focus to an assembly in schools where prayers would seem inappropriate.

Biblical passages relevant to particular units have been listed at the end of the book. These could be used for subsequent assemblies inspiring further thoughts on most of the topics, especially in schools where students are accustomed to hearing readings from the Bible. The Bibliography could also serve as a further resource for the development of themes merely touched upon in the talks.

It is often a struggle to find not only a suitable time but also a place in which to hold regular assemblies. It is my sincere hope that this book may prove helpful to teachers who, engaged in the relentless activity of a school term, must meet in addition to all their other duties the challenge of preparing and conducting an assembly. Many genuinely desire to give guidance to their students, to encourage them to live purposeful lives and to enable them to discover, in the words of the late Cardinal Hume, 'what is truly real', thus setting them firmly on the path from 'now to eternity'.

Attitudes and Beliefs

1. Who Am I?
2. 'I Want to Be Somebody'
3. The Search for Happiness
4. A 'Rabbit Hutch' Existence
5. Order! Order!
6. Pinocchio
7. Dialogue and Definition
8. The Voices of the Page
9. Logs of Wood
10. Controlling the Tongue
11. Godparents
12. The Train Journey
13. Monsignor Quixote
14. To Be a Pilgrim
15. A Box of Bones

1 Who Am I?

'Why is there something rather than just nothing?' This could be a quotation from *Alice in Wonderland* but in fact, it was the type of question posed by Leibniz, a German philosopher and mathematician who lived at the end of the seventeenth and beginning of the eighteenth century. He was born in Leipzig and after holding various court posts, worked as a librarian and historian in Hanover.

The type of question asked by Leibniz is not so very different from the questions we ourselves sometimes ask, although perhaps in rather different words. When we think seriously about it, it is a strange fact that we exist and that we are capable of thinking and reasoning. We might also wonder from time to time why the world exists at all. Has it any purpose or meaning or is it just there? Some people would say that it is pointless to ask such questions because there is no way of answering them; but even if there are no answers, the questions do not go away.

Men and women and children have this capacity for 'wondering' and it is one of the most valuable qualities a human being possesses. If people had not 'wondered' about things and asked probing questions, we would not have advanced along the road of knowledge. Even when we come to the end of what can be known for certain (that is to say, things that can be demonstrated by reason and experience) we still keep 'wondering'. We begin to probe into the unknown, to develop theories of our own and sometimes this leads us to adopt particular beliefs or to adhere to a religious faith. However, even faith or a belief is not just 'a leap into the dark', for most people's convictions take account of all the knowledge available to them as well as of their own experiences.

All the great religions have their own theories about how the world began. Those who, like Christians and Jews, accept the authority of the Hebrew Bible or Old Testament believe that God created the world and has a purpose for it. This does not mean that the early chapters in the Book of Genesis must be taken literally. That the writers of these stories had only rudimentary scientific knowledge and understanding has to be taken into account. [For a more detailed development of these points, see 'The Bible and the Manger, I-II, pages 88-91.] What is really important is not 'how' but 'by whom' and 'why' the world was created. But does the belief that God is the Creator really lead us on to solve the riddle of our existence? What do we, or can we, know about God and his intentions?

It is interesting to note that if someone is prepared to go as far as stating that God created the world, even without understanding 'why' or 'how', that person is at least rejecting another possibility, which is that the world and all that is in it simply came into being by chance. Thus, those who believe that God is the Creator are admitting that there must be some sense in the way things are, or at least, seem to be.

People will inevitably continue to discuss these two opposing theories because they affect the practical business of living. If we believe that there is some overarching purpose in the world and some divine meaning in the scheme of things, then we are more likely to feel at home in God's creation and to have some hope, not only for ourselves but for all humankind, than if we think the appearance of human beings in the world to be accidental.

Seeing the world as God's handiwork, and its creation a caring act, demands 'faith', but having taken that step means recognizing that we as human beings have dignity and identity. If we see ourselves as the objects of God's care, we must have respect not just for ourselves but also for each other and for all God's creatures.

Our whole attitude to life therefore, and to the world as a whole, is affected by our response to that original question: 'Why is there something rather than nothing?'

Thought In the Bible, in the Book of Psalms, the question is posed in another way: 'What is man that you [i.e. God] are mindful of him?'

Prayer Almighty God, who in your wisdom has ordered our earthly life so that we walk by faith and not by sight, correct in us those things in which we are deceived, guide us in things hard to understand, deliver us from untruths and falsehood, until at last, in your perfect light, we see light and gain knowledge of your eternal truth through Jesus Christ our Lord. Amen.

2 'I Want to Be Somebody'

'The Talented Mr Ripley', a highly acclaimed film, was based on a novel about an ambitious young social climber who is a clever musician and mimic, Tom Ripley. Attracted by the lifestyle of an idle rich American, whom, after a violent quarrel, he kills in a fight, Tom assumes the playboy's identity. He roams the great cities of Europe but in order to keep up the deception, he embarks upon one dark deed after another.

This is an extreme case but there are times in life when most people try to project a personality or identity which is not their own. This is often because they are concerned about a particular effect which they want to have on others or because they are anxious to make a good impression. One hears too, from time to time, of someone described as 'a different person' because he or she has moved to fresh surroundings or has acquired a new circle of friends.

Part of the process of growing up is to 'become oneself' by learning to accept one's own limitations, and by discovering and developing the distinctive talents or qualities with which each one of us is endowed. Once this has been achieved, there is no longer a need to project an identity or personality which is not one's own because one will have gained sufficient confidence and courage to be true to oneself.

Michel Quoist, a religious poet, wrote this prayerful poem: 'I Want to Be Somebody', which is concerned with the whole process of 'finding oneself':

Lord, tonight I ask you, once and for all, to rid me of my
Concern about the impression I make on other people.

Forgive me
For being so preoccupied
With what I seem to be,
With the effect I produce
With what others think and say of me.

Forgive me
For wanting to imitate others to the extent that I forget who I am,
For envying their talents so much that I neglect to develop my own.

Forgive me
For the time I spend playing games with my 'personality'
And for the time I don't spend in developing my character

Now, let me forget about the stranger that I was
So that I may find my self;
For I will never know my home unless I leave it,
And I will never find myself if I refuse to lose myself.

Lord, let me be open to my brothers,
So that, through them, you will be able to visit me as your friend.

For then I will be the person that your Love wants me to be,
Your son, Father,
And a brother to my brothers.

Thought In Shakespeare's *Hamlet*, the Lord Chamberlain, Polonius, gives this advice to his son, Laertes:

> *'This above all: to thine own self be true*
> *And it must follow, as the night the day,*
> *Thou canst not then be false to any man.'*
>
> Act I, Scene III

3 The Search for Happiness

In 1998, a young writer called Rachel Cusk won the Somerset Maugham Award for her novel *The Country Life*. The book was praised for its humour, elegant style and emotional honesty. The story describes how Stella, the main character, escaped from the city to a new life in the country. Initially, the title appears fitting, although it gives little indication of the underlying and more significant theme of the novel, which is above all the pursuit of happiness.

Having found work on a farm set in rather remote countryside, the beauty of which Stella greatly appreciated, she soon discovered that life in a small community was not without its problems. It was true that everyone was known and had a place in society but this, in itself, created difficulties because people were far too well informed about the business and daily routine of their neighbours.

There is one passage in the novel which provides the key to the whole story. It records a conversation between Stella and a highly intelligent but severely disabled teenager called Martin. He was the son of a wealthy farmer and his wife, and Stella had been employed by them as his carer. Within a few days of her arrival at the farm, Martin asked Stella whether she was happy. Having already learnt that Martin was skilled at causing trouble, she did not at first reply directly. Although she did not admit it to him, she was rather taken aback by his question and wondered what mischief he meant by it. The conversation, written in the first person singular, continued thus:

> *'Are you?' he repeated.*
>
> *'I suppose so,' I said, settling back in my chair. I was surprised to feel myself on the brink of quite a lengthy reply. 'How would one ever know? I'm as happy as anyone should be, living in a civilized country with no real disadvantages; but whether I am as happy as I could be, I see no way of finding out. I don't happen to think that happiness is the be-all and end-all of everything.'*
>
> *'Then what is?' said Martin.*
>
> *'Oh, I don't know. Coming to an accommodation with oneself, I suppose. Not injuring others. Living a good life. Why ask me?'*
>
> *'Well,' said Martin, putting his large hands on the wheels of his chair and rocking back and forth. 'You did say that you thought happiness wasn't that important. It's an unusual thing to say, Stel-la.'*

'I didn't say that I thought happiness was unimportant. Merely that it wasn't the most important thing. I happen to believe that the search for happiness is often itself the greatest cause of unhappiness.'

'But if you were happy, you wouldn't be searching,' said Martin.

'I didn't say I was. I was speaking generally. I think it is almost impossible to be happy and to know yourself to be so at one and the same time. People believe that happiness is a goal, as opposed merely to the absence of problems. Looking for happiness is like looking for love. How do you know when you've found it?'

'I always imagined they came together,' said Martin.

Thought

Do happiness and love come together?
or
Is it true that 'the search for happiness is often itself the greatest cause of unhappiness'?

It has been said that where charity and love are, there is God. What do you think this means?

Prayer

O Lord, stir the hearts of all your people that they may increase their efforts to promote the cause of charity and love, and by their good works lead many to praise and glorify your holy name. Amen.

4 A 'Rabbit Hutch' Existence

We once had a rabbit which lived in a hutch outside the back door, and in rabbit years, it lived to be quite elderly. By nature, the rabbit was placid and totally lacking in initiative. It was extremely difficult to persuade it to leave its hutch and when we did encourage it to do so, it always seemed anxious to return. When the hutch was being cleaned, it sat quietly in a cardboard box, making no attempt to eat the surrounding grass or to escape into the nearby undergrowth. When the cleaning process had been completed, it jumped back gratefully into its familiar surroundings.

One morning, we found that because we had been careless and had not closed the hutch door properly, the hutch was empty. We searched in the undergrowth and in the neighbouring field but found no rabbit; so we assumed that it had escaped and at last discovered the joys of freedom. But we were mistaken because, returning from the search, we found it cowering in an empty hutch - next door to its own - a hutch once inhabited by its sister rabbit.

It seemed that the only lifestyle our rabbit could appreciate and enjoy was life confined within a wooden box - and even when given the opportunity to experience freedom and a fuller life, it refused to take advantage of the offer. It could have added another dimension to its existence by enjoying the real world of the undergrowth and grass which grew beyond the wire netting of its hutch but it had no desire to do so. The real world, as far as our rabbit was concerned, was the hutch. What to us seems real was for the rabbit the unknown, the unfamiliar, the mysterious and therefore unreal.

The rabbit thought, if it thought at all, 'I'm not taking the risk of moving into the unfamiliar and the mysterious. I would rather feel secure. Beyond my hutch, life would be uncertain and difficult.'

We can't really blame the rabbit for thinking in this way, for many people have a similar attitude to life. They too live lives which are totally enclosed by the walls of the world which they know - filling their days with familiar interests, never looking beyond their immediate work, their leisure activities, their sport and their friends, never taking the opportunity to find a new dimension to their lives perhaps by asking a few significant questions: Why am I here? What is the purpose of this life? Why do I exist - if I exist at all? Is there a God? If so, what difference does it make to me - or to the world?

In asking such questions, we may well find that we have to consider the possibility of another dimension to our lives or be led to conclude that the life we are leading at present is like the life of the rabbit within the hutch - narrow and restricting. We may even discover that reality lies in the world beyond the 'wire-netting' - in the mysterious or the spiritual, or in what the Bible calls 'eternity', rather than in the world limited by time and space, so that even time is not as important as we once thought.

Someone once asked the late Cardinal Hume this question: 'If I were to explore the idea of mystery and God, would I not be moving into the world of dreams and escaping from what is real?' The Cardinal answered: 'No, this is not so. To explore mystery is to discover what is truly real.'

From this, we could conclude that it seems important to show a little more curiosity and initiative than the rabbit - by exploring the mysterious world beyond the rabbit hutch of our existence. Such exploration does however take time and thought, so it is vital to avoid becoming like another rabbit - the white rabbit in *Alice in Wonderland*, who had no time for anything. Unlike our rabbit, he hurried from one activity to another, constantly taking a watch out of his waistcoat pocket, saying 'Oh dear! Oh dear! I shall be too late,' or 'No time No time!'

So in our lives, we need to take care that we are not so obsessed by time that we lose sight of eternity, nor must we be so restricted by our worldly activities that we fail, in the words of Cardinal Hume, 'to catch sight of what is truly real', or, if you like, what lies beyond the rabbit hutch of our existence.

Thought Do you lead a 'rabbit hutch' existence? In what ways could you broaden your outlook and interests?

Prayer Prevent us, O Lord, from being so obsessed by the pursuit of worldly things that we fail to grow in the knowledge of your heavenly reality. Amen.

5 Order! Order!

'Bilgewater' was the nickname of Marigold Green, who grew up in the boys' school where her father taught. To his pupils, he was known as 'Bill' and Marigold, whose mother died when she was born, was always referred to as 'Bill's daughter' or more commonly by the nickname given to her by the boys: 'Bilgewater'. She is the main character of an entertaining and striking novel by Jane Gardam, a novelist who has won two Whitbread awards as well as being a runner-up for the Booker Prize.

In this particular novel called *Bilgewater*, Marigold describes herself as 'hideous, quaint and barmy' because she is convinced of her own plainness and peculiarity. As the story progresses, readers find themselves viewing the world through the eyes of Marigold and from the stance of her unusual upbringing. Much to her own surprise, she found leaving school a terrible shock and admits that she had not really come to terms with the fact that once her A levels were over, school would be over too for ever. Marigold expresses her feelings about this vividly and in so doing, gives a picture of life in her own school, which may or may not be similar to yours and to your own experiences of school life.

> *All those years and years of bells. Such an age and age of school. Those preps and speech days and Aileen Sykes and Miss Bex. The awful gym lessons. The terrible dinners. The smelly lavatories. The frightful, pitiless games of hockey with me always running the wrong way. The sniggers, the friendlessness. But at the same time the pattern, the plot, the safety was now gone. The plans all made for you, the security of knowing that on Monday come wind or high water you would have to be doing Double Applied. That if anyone wanted you in a hurry they would know for certain you would be in Room Eight, over the Quad. The sureness of what to do next. The sureness that you were not just wasting your time because you had no choice in the matter anyway. The sureness that free time was precious and that the sands and the sea and the park and the garden had heavenly properties because, like heaven, they were except at certain moments forbidden and inaccessible. Now I was utterly free.*

While at school, Marigold had longed for a release from the strict and rigid routine but once it came, she found that the prospect of freedom and choice was unexpectedly frightening. The pattern and plot of the school timetable, which had given her security, was no longer there. She herself was now responsible for finding a new pattern and a new plot for her life, which was now under her own control. It was up to her to create her own distinctive lifestyle and that, as she and most people discover, is not easy when given such freedom and choice for the first time.

There are two key words which have to be kept in mind when faced with this situation: one is 'freedom' and the other is 'order'.

Von Balthasar, a philosopher and theologian who died at the end of the last century, attempted through his prolific writings to encourage people to observe the importance of beauty and order and balance when they looked at the world in its entirety. Like conservationists, he was convinced that the balance of nature should not be disturbed. He believed too in the equal yet distinctive roles of men and women in society. He feared that in the present era of technology – a time which he described as both 'motherless and fatherless' – men and women suffer from a sense of insecurity because they are confused and uncertain about their distinctive roles. 'If we do not look at society and at the aims of that society as a whole', he wrote, 'we lose our sense of balance and the importance of the interdependence of one group upon another.'

Von Balthasar's ideas also have important implications for the life of each individual. An orderly existence results from a way of life which maintains a balance between, for example, freedom and discipline, work and leisure, tradition and novelty. Once released from the routine of school, college or even home, if balance and order are lacking in our lives, we lose control. Consequently, as Marigold Green realized, without a pattern or plot for our lives, we have no real sense of security.

Thought

And let our ordered lives confess
the beauty of thy peace.

These are two lines from a hymn often sung at school assemblies. What is the connection between 'order' and 'peace'?

6 Pinocchio

In the cemetery of the ancient monastery of San Miniato in Florence, there is amongst the gravestones one which is inscribed, in huge letters, with the name 'Pinocchio'.

This was pointed out to me by Dom Domingo, a young Italian monk with a great sense of humour. He was amused by my bewilderment because as far as I was concerned, it was like showing me the grave of 'Cinderella' or 'Red Riding Hood' or some other fairy-tale figure. Not knowing any Italian, I was unable to translate the other words inscribed on the stone. Eventually the monk explained in his halting English that the grave was, in fact, that of the man who wrote the story of the puppet Pinocchio – now immortalized by Walt Disney.

Sometimes when we look at puppets, even very ordinary ones, for they do not have to be special like Pinocchio, it is easy to imagine that they have wills and minds of their own. When watching a Punch and Judy show for example, it is natural for children (and adults for that matter) to identify with what they imagine are the 'feelings' of the puppets. The audience will join in the dialogue, express concern and even answer questions which are put to them. It is so easy to forget that without the hands and voice of the human being behind the scenes, Punch and Judy are lifeless dolls.

Sadly, many people in this life become rather like puppets, simply because they are not prepared to think for themselves. They are completely swayed by public opinion or the media, controlled by the dictates of fashion and interested only in the pursuits enjoyed by the majority of their contemporaries. Yet as people, we are all different, each one of us with a mind capable of independent thought. Each one of us has a variety of talents and skills which need to be developed in a distinctive way. Unlike puppets, we are not controlled by strings. We have freedom, God-given freedom (according to the Bible), to choose and to act independently.

Recently, on a University Open Day, a lecturer described what he expected of the students he hoped to admit to his course. Undoubtedly, he wanted candidates with good GCSE and A-level results but that was by no means the only qualifying factor. He hoped, he explained, for students who could think for themselves, who would probe and question, taking nothing for granted and who could argue logically, thus sharpening the minds of those who taught them. He would welcome, he added, candidates with original interests and with enthusiasm for aspects of their chosen subject not necessarily covered by the examination syllabus. In other words, he did not want 'puppets'.

So when you next adjust your 'Walkman' ask yourself whether you are listening to a tape or CD just because everyone else is playing it. When next you switch on the television to watch indiscriminately, ask yourself whether the time could be spent more profitably. Perhaps, for example, developing a new interest would help to exercise your mind and make you a livelier and more mature person.

It is worth remembering that personalities have to be developed and minds have to be fed. Growth in these two areas is a long, slow process and such growth cannot be fostered too soon. Unlike puppets, people do not reach their full potential as soon as you pull the strings.

Thought Are you conscious of the development of your own personality? Can you identify your own strengths and weaknesses?

Prayer Help us, O Lord, to realize our full potential and to make use of the talents and skills with which you have endowed us, that they may be used in your service and to the benefit of our fellow human beings. Amen.

7 Dialogue and Definition

In any school or college, a variety of views is held by staff and students on every subject under the sun. This is inevitable in any community. One would hope though that these opinions are based not merely on prejudice but on a serious consideration of any matter which happens to be under discussion.

A subject over which there will certainly be a division of opinion is on the significance of the events commemorated on Good Friday and Easter Sunday. Some will see the crucified Jesus as an object of pity. They will feel regret that he was made to suffer and die undeservedly but the resurrection narratives they will dismiss as 'idle tales', just as the disciples did, when they first heard rumours of Jesus' appearances after his death. Those who hold this view will then, without further thought, make plans for the two bank holidays. Others will remember the events of these two days with the eye of faith, in which case for them, the crucifixion and resurrection of Jesus will provide many of the answers they seek about the meaning of life and death. Briefly then, it is possible to see in the cross what fallen human nature can do to another human being, and in addition, it is possible to see in the cross what Christ can do for fallen human nature. In all educational institutions, both points of view will be represented. What matters, however, is not so much the differences of opinion but whether the conclusions have been reached as a result of informed and honest thinking.

Real conviction must never be based on mere sentiment or emotion. It is essential that those who believe the cross and resurrection to be the two most significant events in history, should have thought through the reason for their faith. It is equally important that those who maintain that the crucifixion and resurrection of Jesus have no relevance in the third millennium have also reached their conclusions with intellectual honesty. St Paul, who was himself a man of intellect, understood that for many, both Greeks and Jews, the cross of Christ seemed 'foolishness' and a 'stumbling block', certainly not a fact upon which one would expect to base a religion. Those, however, who see in the cross the 'power and wisdom of God' have no authority to sit in judgement upon those who do not. Many of the latter have not come to their conclusions lightly and have great respect for those who are able to embrace the Christian faith.

Christians themselves can learn much not just from those of other faiths but also from their agnostic, atheist or humanist friends, who are sometimes more sensitive about the problems of their fellow human beings. They are generally more willing to give time and energy to charitable causes, while sadly, many Christians are too inward looking, too concerned with their own spiritual progress and with the problems in their own Churches, such as falling numbers or over-large buildings. They also tend to forget that God, who is omnipotent and omniscient, must surely work out his purposes through both those who have faith in him and those who do not.

In the Bible, we find that it was Pharaoh's daughter who rescued Moses when, as a baby, he was hidden in his cradle amongst the reeds at the river bank by his mother. Although he grew up under the influence of the Egyptian court, he was aware of his Hebrew origins, for the Egyptian princess unknowingly had employed his mother as his nurse. Eventually, under Moses' leadership, the Jews miraculously escaped from Egypt and this 'Exodus' is regarded as the most significant event in the history of the Jewish nation. It was, however, brought about by God through Moses, who owed his life to one who had no faith in God and to one who did. Likewise, in St Luke's account of the nativity of Jesus, it was a decree of Caesar Augustus, the Roman Emperor, that 'all the world should be taxed', which caused Mary and Joseph to be in Bethlehem for the birth of Jesus. Thus, Christians believe, an Old Testament prophecy was fulfilled by the action of a secular ruler.

So, as St Paul realized, Christians have no cause for boasting about their faith, which is a gift from God and not something they have achieved for themselves. God, who is a universal God, can work through whomsoever he chooses, through unbelievers as well as those who profess Christianity or another religious faith.

It is therefore essential in any centre of study not to be narrow-minded but to engage in dialogue with others whose opinions may be different from our own. It is only by entering into such discussions that we can clarify our own opinions and define them and as a result, we can learn to explain them more effectively and think about our reasons for upholding them. Thus, without dialogue, there can be no definition and without definition, there can be no conviction.

Prayer

Almighty God, our heavenly Father
Without whose light, search is in vain;
Invigorate our studies and direct our enquiries,
That we may pursue them with diligence and right discernment...
Let us not linger in ignorance
But enlighten and support us;
For the sake of Jesus Christ our Lord. Amen.

FROM A PRAYER COMPOSED BY DR JOHNSON (1709–1786)

Even in this age of computers, word processors and videos, books are still important. At times, your lockers will not shut properly because they contain too many books. Often too, you can scarcely bear the weight of them in your bags and brief-cases and sometimes, in the library, you try to write your essays surrounded by so many books that you scarcely know how or where to begin.

Books these days are such commonplace things. There are recipe books in the kitchen, guidebooks for the holidays, books about sport, the garden and every hobby imaginable. We extend our bookcases in order to accommodate the books we have accumulated and yet so many of them remain on our shelves unread.

Consider for a moment how different things were when books were written or copied by hand.

To make a single book, a whole flock of sheep was often required in order to produce enough skins for the parchment. You could not get many pages from one sheepskin. Wild animals too had to be hunted if there were insufficient domestic animals to produce leather for the binding. It took weeks to make the leather ready for use and even after careful preparation, the parchment always offered some resistance to the quill or the pen.

A medieval monk spent years writing or copying one book. Progress in the winter was especially slow in the draughty cloisters of a monastery where fingers suffered from severe cold and the ink was often frozen.

The completion of a book was a great event - and just as a new church building was dedicated with special prayers, so a book, when finished, was offered to God at a special ceremony with suitable prayers.

'Accept, O Holy Trinity, the offering of this book', the monks chanted in Latin and then they prayed for the brethren who had prepared the parchment or leather, for the monk who had done the writing and copying, for those who would read the book, and for those who, in future generations, would one day own it.

To have written or copied a book was certainly considered as important as designing or building a church. In some ways, it was a greater achievement.

The church building would serve only the local community but the effect of a book could be far reaching. An abbot of the great monastery at Cluny, Peter the Venerable, once wrote:

In the furrows traced by a monk on a parchment, he will sow the seeds of divine words ... he will preach without opening his mouth; without breaking his silence, he will make the Lord's teaching resound in the ears of the nations and, without leaving the monastery, he will journey over land and sea.

The fact that books required so much time and effort to produce meant that they were valued possessions and you had to make the most of those which were available. Consequently, as you read a book, you gave it your whole attention. Reading involved speaking, listening, thinking and remembering. Your eyes saw the words, your mouth pronounced them aloud, your ears listened to the words which the monks called 'the voices of the page', your memory fixed and understood the words and your will desired to put into practice what you had learnt from the words.

Doctors in ancient and medieval times used to recommend reading as a physical exercise - on an equal level with walking, running or playing games. Reading, it was claimed, exercised the body and the mind - one learnt with one's whole being.

The library of a medieval monastery contained classical texts as well as religious books. Any scholarly text was looked upon with great reverence. It was the custom on Ash Wednesday for abbots to issue their monks with books for their Lent reading. Often there were not enough religious books to go around and there is a delightful story about one monk who found himself with Livy's *History of Rome* for his Lenten reading. Disappointed, he explained to his abbot that he did not think such a book would help his spiritual progress. 'My son,' the Abbot replied, 'do you believe that God is the source of all truth?' 'That I do believe,' said the monk. 'Then,' said the Abbot, 'all scholarly books contain God's truth and you will find moral and spiritual lessons in Livy, as well as in the Book of Leviticus, if you are prepared to search for them. The revelations of God's truth cannot be restricted to the Scriptures.' So from this, we gather that in the Middle Ages, the work of a genuine scholar in any field of study was read appreciatively as the work of the Holy Spirit.

A medieval scholar, then, involved his whole being when reading his books - for his reading did not merely inform him, but formed him. His reflective reading affected and helped the formation of his character - and all the learning acquired through reading in this way was offered to the service of God, like the books from which it had been derived. These medieval methods of study are strange to us. Men and women of the twenty-first century cannot ignore the eight hundred years of development in methods of education and the new scientific ways of thinking which separate us from medieval times, yet we can learn something from medieval scholars.

Learning, they maintained, required total concentration. Such concentration certainly cannot be achieved against the background of radio or television - or at the same time as chewing gum or eating crisps, or with one eye on the clock.

Reading and learning with 'the whole being' could have quite an effect on the quality of the work which we produce and even on our personalities - and if we also felt that, like the monk, we could offer our learning to the service of God, who knows what the result might be!

Thought In a world which is so full of distractions, is it still possible to develop the art of total concentration?

Prayer Direct, O God, our studies, and grant that the knowledge we gain through them may be used in the service of your world to bring about your eternal purpose through Jesus Christ our Lord. Amen.

9 Logs of Wood

Recently, in a shop in Cambridge, I found a birthday card which greatly interested me, although it may not have appealed to the person who received it.

The design covered both front and back of the card and was composed of rows and rows of logs of wood, chopped up into different shapes and sizes and arranged so that the grain of the wood was uppermost. What particularly attracted me to the card was the number of different patterns contained in the wood grain, demonstrating that the logs must have been cut from a variety of trees.

Those logs of wood became even more significant to me as a result of visiting, later in the day, a friend who lives in a tall but very narrow Georgian house in one of the back streets of Cambridge. The house has four floors, each with two small rooms approached from minute landings at each stage of a winding staircase. As I was led into the sitting-room on the first floor, my attention was drawn to the shape of the door. It curved inwards in order to give just a little more space on the landing to people who laboriously climbed the steep staircase. Only an eighteenth-century craftsman, I thought, would have taken the trouble to have produced such a beautifully curved and panelled door. Just imagine how much time and patience it must have taken to make.

The wood would have been carefully treated before it was used. The panels then cut to size, soaked, put into a clamp, which would have been tightened a little more each day until there was the right amount of curve to enable the door to fit into the available space.

But what is the point of describing a birthday card, logs of wood and a curved door? The point is that the card showed wood in its natural state, every log different, untreated, unpolished but nevertheless potentially useful; while the door demonstrated what can be done with wood when it has undergone these processes and has been fitted together with other similar pieces. Once this has been achieved, it can serve a useful purpose.

The same contrast can be seen in us. We begin life rather like logs of wood, roughly hewn, all shapes, all sizes, with different patterns of grain - or in our own case, talents and gifts. Gradually, however, we are shaped by the discipline imposed upon us by parents and teachers and by the influence of the communities in which we live. We are also encouraged to work and co-operate with others so that we can lead useful lives.

Christ himself, as a carpenter's son, understood this process. In a very special way he worked and still works, not with wood but with people who will allow him to do so. Just as a carpenter has the vision to see what could be produced from a plank or log of wood, so Christ sees our potential and what each of us could achieve. Allowing the 'Divine Carpenter' to shape our lives is not always comfortable because being cut down to size and accepting that our own lives are not at the centre of the universe never is. It is a humbling experience but it is certainly worthwhile in that we become aware that we can then play a small but vital part in working out God's purpose for the world.

Thought

A favourite prayer of John Wesley, the founder of the Methodist movement, was: 'Lord, let me not live to be useless.'

How would you define a 'useful life? Is 'usefulness' something which you are taking into account when considering a career?

10 Controlling the Tongue

There is in the Bible, one Epistle or Letter which was amongst the last batch of books to be included. In fact, it was not until the very end of the fourth century that Church leaders eventually decided that it should be regarded as 'a book of Holy Scripture'. Even so, there were those in later history who regretted its inclusion. Amongst them was Martin Luther, a famous early-sixteenth-century scholar, who by the way, was also responsible for writing what is probably the best-known Christmas carol, 'Away in a Manger'.

Martin Luther called the controversial letter 'a right strawy epistle', in other words, a letter of straw, worthless. The letter to which I am referring, as those of you who are studying the Reformation period in your history lessons will already have guessed, is the letter attributed to James, who describes himself as 'a servant of God and of the Lord Jesus Christ'.

Why was his letter considered so dubious? The main reason was the way in which the writer explained one aspect of Christian teaching. In so doing he appeared to be contradicting the Apostle St Paul. It was not, however, that the two writers held conflicting views but merely that they stressed different points. Each was commenting on the faults and shortcomings of the group of Christians to whom they were writing and as one would expect, not every Christian community had exactly the same weaknesses.

St Paul was inspired to stress the importance of faith, because he was aware that the Christians in some of the Churches he had established were putting too much trust in their own actions, their own good deeds, rather than in God's mercy. This was particularly true of the Christians in Rome and to them, St Paul had to explain that it was faith alone which enabled them to deepen their relationship with God. He pointed out, however, that this did not mean that they could behave as they liked because their faith in God should result in Christian standards of morality. Actions were also important.

James, on the other hand, was writing for Christians who were outwardly expressing their faith but were not allowing it to influence their behaviour - a necessary consequence of any profession of faith, whatever your religion. 'Be doers of the word and not hearers only, deceiving yourselves,' warned James. It is surprising that there was so much disagreement about this epistle because Jesus himself had expressed a similar view in the Sermon on the Mount: 'Not everyone who says to me "Lord, Lord" shall enter the kingdom of heaven; but he who does the will of my Father who is in heaven.' (Matthew 7:21)

We can see from all this that the teaching of James did not differ radically from that of St Paul. It was good that the Church eventually decided to include the Letter of James in the Bible because it contains extremely useful advice, especially about the control of the tongue, for example:

If any one thinks he is religious and does not bridle his tongue but deceives his heart, this man's religion is vain.

JAMES 1:26

The tongue is a little member and boasts of great things. How great a forest is set ablaze by a small fire! And the tongue is a fire ... For every kind of beast and bird, of reptile and sea creature, can be tamed and has been tamed by humankind but no human being can tame the tongue - a restless evil, full of deadly poison.

JAMES 3:5-8

Thought Why is it so difficult to 'tame the tongue'?

Prayer God be in my mouth and in my speaking.

Godparents

If you happen to have godparents, you may well wonder why your parents, who were responsible for selecting them, chose the people they did. So often, after the christening and the first few years of childhood, godparents tend to disappear from the scene. Sometimes they move away from the locality in which you live or your own family moves house, so it is not easy for them to remain in close contact with their godchildren. Others, and this is more often the case, forget about the promises they made at the christening and the responsibilities they undertook for the spiritual welfare of their godchildren. So for many young people, godparents are a 'dead loss', which is a great pity, for their main task, to help to inform their godchildren about the Christian faith, is an important one.

Fortunately however, there are some who take their responsibilities seriously - the godfather of one of our sons, for example, was all that a godfather should be. Not only was he generous (and from the godchild's point of view, I know that this is important) but he also took a genuine interest in every aspect of his godson's life and his spiritual development. He really tried to understand him and often with more success than his natural parents. This godfather visited regularly, telephoned from time to time and frequently wrote lively and amusing letters, which contained cleverly disguised, sound advice. Sadly, he died just at the time when he was most appreciated. The letters however, which he had written over the years, were carefully kept and I have permission to quote from one of them.

This particular letter was sent at the time when his godson was embarking upon the round of interviews which are necessary if one is aiming to gain a university place. This is a process with which some of you are already familiar and which some of you will certainly experience in the near future. The advice in this letter is sound and worthy of your consideration whether or not you are planning to go to university.

Dear Andrew

Just a word to wish you all good fortune in your assault upon the universities. It is uncanny how, without any influence on my part, you go along a similar track to me.

I am sure that if you are a normal candidate, you will look around at the others who have also been called for interview and feel despair, since everyone else looks and appears so learned and intelligent. One perhaps will be the widely travelled son of an ambassador, who already speaks six languages. Another may claim (although you do not have to believe him) that he is a chess grand master who wrote Greek verse for his father on his sixth birthday - highly unlikely these days - but you may as well be prepared for the most extraordinary claims on the part of other candidates, who could undermine your confidence. Then, there are the women, many, many more than in my day and all of them, the best, at least having what Keats called 'a passionate intensity'.

It is important to remember that this experience is mutual, universal, timeless ...

Above all, never fear the result of failure. Nearly all the best things in life which have happened to me, have been the result of disappointment rather than success. Hard to bear at the time but you will find in the long run that I am right, although it has taken my whole life to confirm it.

One important point - interviewers and examiners are not enemies to be bashed, much less fools to be hoodwinked, so do not (by name dropping at your interview) try to give the impression that you know more than you do. It stands out a mile to a college lecturer or university don. Have sufficient confidence in yourself to wind down before you tackle an interview or an examination and take courage, my friend - 'le diable est mort!'

Thought

Have you ever experienced in your life a disappointment which proved in the long run to be beneficial?

Prayer

In times of doubt and despondency, O Lord, give us courage and the guidance of your divine wisdom. Prevent us from making wrong choices and enable us to seek to do your will through Jesus Christ our Lord. Amen.

12 The Train Journey

I wonder how many of you have travelled a really long distance by train. It can be exceedingly boring but so often the enjoyment of the journey is made or marred by the other passengers in whose company you find yourself. The variety of people who climb on and off a train at station-stops is intriguing and can be a source of great amusement, or sometimes, a cause for irritation.

Once, not so very long ago, I boarded the Penzance to Paddington train in order to go to Reading. As my journey began at Penzance, I had nearly five hours in which to observe my fellow passengers. Sitting opposite me at first was a schoolboy, who from an enormous black canvas bag, produced a mathematics textbook, an exercise book and after a considerable amount of rummaging, a pencil case and calculator. He then painstakingly arranged and rearranged in a variety of patterns, his pens, pencils and other equipment. Eventually, he began what I presumed was his homework, although it was completed in far less time than the elaborate preparatory process. When he left the train, his seat was taken by an elderly businessman, who hid behind the *Financial Times* all the way to Exeter. Finally, I was joined by an attractive young woman, armed with her 'Walkman', a magazine and a packet of polos. She spent most of the journey filing her fingernails, at least until we reached Reading, which was my station-stop.

A train journey is, in so many ways, a parable of life. Life on the planet goes on and on like a train moving to its destination, regardless of who is sitting inside it. Each of us is like a passenger, who enters the train for a limited length of time, some people for a short time, others for longer because the span of our lives is variable and unpredictable. No matter how long or how short a period we, as individuals, have in this world, life on the planet continues. Just as a driver guides a train to its destination, so God (many people believe) works out his overall purpose for the world - a purpose that is being worked through the ages, before we entered the world, while we live within it and after we have left it.

On life's journey, there are three types of passenger. There are those who pursue their own interests, rather like the schoolboy, the businessman and the young woman I observed on my journey. Secondly, there are those who are perfect menaces to their fellow travellers. They talk incessantly, complain loudly, place their luggage in the gangways where others trip over it and leave behind them empty coffee cups, drinks tins, sticky sweet-wrappings and torn newspapers. Even those who join the train at a later stage are affected by their inconsiderate behaviour. Thirdly, there are those passengers who are constantly aware of the needs of others. They carry cases for the elderly, fetch tea or coffee for mothers with small children and when they leave he train, they dispose of their litter in a waste bin or take it with them. Such people make the journey pleasanter both for those who travel with them and for those who come after them.

You do not, in fact, have to make a railway journey to find these three types of people. You will spot them in any school or college, workplace, factory or office. There are those who do not wish to get involved with the lives of others and their problems. Secondly, there are those selfish and demanding types who constantly draw attention to themselves and who have no social consciences whatsoever. Thirdly, there are the genuinely public-spirited people who are prepared to put others before themselves, even to their own cost. It is through the lives of the latter, who love their neighbours as themselves, that God is best able to fulfil his purpose for the world.

Thought

God is working his purpose out
As year succeeds to year.

Two lines from a well-known hymn. Can you see any evidence supporting this belief?

Prayer

Oh Lord, our God, inspire and strengthen us by the Holy Spirit that by word and good example, we may devote ourselves wholly to your service, and so fulfil your purpose for the world for the glory of your name; through Jesus Christ our Lord. Amen.

13 Monsignor Quixote

[This assembly may be abridged by omitting the section following the asterisks and using the second 'thought' or second prayer if desired.]

Monsignor Quixote is a novel by the Roman Catholic writer Graham Greene. It is a story which blends humour with sharp insight, or in the words of one reviewer, 'a mixture of entertainment and deep human awareness'. In the film version produced for Thames Television, Alec Guinness starred as Monsignor Quixote.

The novel describes the travels of an elderly Spanish priest and an ex-Mayor, who is a Communist. Together, they set off from a remote Spanish village, where they had lived for thirty years and which they had rarely left, in order to explore modern Spain. The novel begins with a description of the priest's ancient car in which they travelled.

There was no air-conditioning in his little Seat 600 which he had bought, already second hand, eight years before. As he drove he thought sadly of the day when he would have to find a new car. A dog's years can be multiplied by seven to equal a man's, and by that calculation his car would still be in early middle age, but he noticed how already his parishioners began to regard his Seat as almost senile. 'You can't trust it, Don Quixote,' they would warn him and he could only reply. 'It has been with me through many bad days, and I pray God that it may survive me.' So many of his prayers had remained unanswered that he had hopes that this one prayer of his had lodged all the time like wax in the Eternal ear.

Most of the novel's narrative is in the form of a dialogue between the priest and the Mayor, who gently tease each other about their respective beliefs. One thing, however, they find they have in common and that is that each shared from time to time a sense of doubt.

'The idea of Hell has sometimes disturbed my sleeplessness,' admitted the priest to the Mayor on one occasion. 'Perhaps,' he continued, 'that same night in your room you are thinking ... Was Stalin - or Lenin - necessarily right? I hope - friend - that you sometimes doubt too. It's human to doubt.'
'I try not to doubt,' the Mayor said.
'Oh, so do I. So do I,' said the priest 'in that we are certainly alike.'

***

The author then goes on to describe how the priest mused upon the fact that sharing a sense of doubt could bring men together, even more than sharing a belief. With these thoughts still very much in mind, the priest during his siesta had a terrible dream, which stayed with him 'like a cheap tune in his head'.

> *He had dreamt that Christ had been saved from the Cross by the legion of angels to which on an earlier occasion the Devil had told Him that He could appeal. So there was no final agony, no heavy stone which had to be rolled away, no discovery of an empty tomb. Father Quixote stood there watching on Golgotha as Christ stepped down from the cross triumphant and acclaimed. The Roman soldiers, even the Centurion, knelt in His honour, and the people of Jerusalem poured up the hill to worship Him. The disciples clustered happily around. His mother smiled through her tears of joy. There was no ambiguity, no room for doubt and no room for faith at all. The whole world knew with certainty that Christ was the Son of God.*
>
> *It was only a dream, of course it was only a dream, but none the less Father Quixote had felt on waking the chill of despair felt by a man who realizes suddenly that he has taken up a profession which is of use to no one, who must continue to live in a kind of Saharan desert without doubt or faith, where everyone is certain that the same belief is true. He had found himself whispering. 'God save me from such a belief.' Then he heard the Mayor turn restlessly on the bed beside him, and he added without thought, 'Save him too from belief,' and only then he fell asleep again.*

Through his dream, the priest had realized that without the final agony, the death and resurrection of Christ, the Christian faith would not have survived. A faith based upon the 'crucified' Christ has often been ridiculed. In the early days of Christianity, St Paul was well aware of this. 'Christ crucified,' he wrote in one of his letters, was 'a stumbling block to the Jews and foolishness to the Gentiles' but to those who are called to the faith, he concluded, 'it is the power of God.' Don Quixote, as a result of his dream, came to a similar conclusion. He, like St Paul, began to understand that it was through the crucifixion that one becomes aware of the power and wisdom of God at work, and that without the resurrection, there would be no way of demonstrating that death was not the end. There would be no mystery to be revealed, no need for faith, no room for doubt.

St Paul admitted that if Christ had not been raised from the dead, his preaching would have been in vain, and now, Don Quixote had also learnt that without a crucified and risen Christ, his priestly work would have been of no use to anyone.

The suffering of Christ, and indeed, the problem of pain and suffering in general, is something we all find baffling and impossible to explain - especially if we believe that God is a God of love. That very belief, however, may be more closely associated with suffering than it at first appears; for if God is a loving God, suffering is inevitable. Why is this? It is because genuine love for others or for another always involves self-sacrifice, suffering, hurt or inconvenience. Not to put oneself first is never easy.

'Our suffering is as great as our love … as is our love, so is our suffering,' wrote Heloise in a letter to the twelfth-century scholar Peter Abelard. So perhaps we should conclude: 'as was Christ's love (for us) so was his suffering.'

This may not answer our question but it does at least encourage us to think positively about the problem.

Thought Jesus said, 'Greater love has no man than this that he lays down his life for his friends.' (John 15:13) Can you think of examples of such sacrifice in modern life?

or

Thought 'Faith which does not doubt is dead faith.' Do you agree?

Prayer O God, help us to reflect your love in our lives by bearing one another's burdens through Jesus Christ our Lord. Amen.

or

Prayer O Lord, our God, we pray for all those who have lost their faith in you and who suffer from doubt and despondency. Support and strengthen them with your grace that they may recover their faith in you, and lead their lives confident of your eternal providence through Jesus Christ our Lord. Amen.

To Be a Pilgrim

The late Cardinal Hume (Archbishop of Westminster) began one of his books with this paragraph.

> *Life,* he wrote, *is a pilgrimage. We are on the march and sooner or later, we shall reach our destination. Then we shall see God as he is and that experience will be the cause of happiness and will have no end.*

That was all very well for Cardinal Hume, for he had made up his mind about the purpose of life and if he had not believed in God, he would not have been made Archbishop of Westminster – but what about the rest of us?

There is no doubt that for all of us, life is a kind of pilgrimage but many spend their time on the road in some confusion and therefore do not make much progress. Some eventually come to the conclusion that there is no God, others go through life with severe doubts and therefore have difficulty in finding their way. Some, however, seem to forge ahead with such certainty about the faith they profess that it can be off-putting to others unless they share the same conviction. But in whatever position we find ourselves, important questions do have to be asked. Why am I here? What is the meaning of life? Are we part of a universe devoid of sense or purpose? If there is a God, what is he like and what does he require of us?

If, of course, we could *see* God, we would not need to ask these questions and life would be different. It would be easy to believe and we should be able to take the next step on our pilgrimage, clear about the direction. In fact, faith would be unnecessary because it would have 'vanished into sight'. We have to accept, however, that in our present life, this is not the case.

Furthermore, because we are unable to *see* God, it is all too easy to push any thoughts about him or about the purpose of life to the backs of our minds. We become engrossed with all kinds of interests so that often we are so busy working, enjoying ourselves or tired that important questions remain unasked. At other times, we are so horrified by the innocent sufferings of others in times of earthquake, famine or as a result of accidents, that we dismiss any idea of a God who loves us and who leads us to a destination where we shall experience, in the words of the late Cardinal Hume, 'the cause of happiness.'

Yet, if we do dismiss religion completely, we miss out on one important aspect of life, the spiritual dimension. Religious believers would say that our lives are then impoverished and pointless, with no ultimate future or destination to which we can look forward. Whenever pilgrims or travellers lose their way, they stop to think and to reconsider before they decide on the next step. There are times when it would be wise for us to follow their example and take a similar course of action.

There is a well-known story about three headteachers discussing the kind of education they were aiming to give their pupils. The first claimed that he was training his to become law-abiding citizens. The second explained that she was preparing hers to be public spirited and of service to the community.

The third gave a very simple answer. 'Preparing them for death,' he said quietly, 'for death is the only certainty in life.'

In Angela Huth's novel *The Wives of Fishermen*, a fisherman's widow visits the fish market. The writer describes how, when the woman looks at the dead fish,

> *She sees how in death every one is different. Some look resigned. Some are still open mouthed in indignation. Some have a chinless, weary look as if the catastrophe of being caught in the net was of no consequence.*

This paragraph raises the whole question of how death should be approached. With resignation? With indignation? With indifference? Or is there another, more positive way, which the late Cardinal Hume not only wrote about but also demonstrated?

Thought Should our attitude to life determine our attitude to death or should our attitude to death determine our attitude to life? Why? What might be the effects on people's lives of these different approaches?

Prayer

Lord, it belongs not to my care
Whether I die or live;
To love and serve thee is my share
And this, thy grace must give. Amen.

RICHARD BAXTER (1615–1691)

A Box of Bones

Which of your possessions would you attempt to save in the event of a fire? I would certainly not risk my life for a small wooden box which I would hope to rescue, but I would be extremely sorry to lose it. Neither the box nor its contents have any monetary value. It simply contains a few brittle, crumbling bones. 'Are they human bones?' you may be thinking and the answer is 'yes'. 'But whose?' you ask, and that I am afraid I am unable to answer. However, I can explain how they were acquired and why I value them so highly.

Hidden in the sand dunes of the north coast of Cornwall is the ruin of a little Celtic church. Guidebooks describe it as the remains of a fifth-century monastery associated with one of the most notable of Cornish saints, St Piran. The books also point out that on the south side of the church, there is evidence of a burial ground and that because of the constantly shifting sands, human bones, bits of skull and even teeth rise to the surface and can be excavated by gently sifting the sand.

Growing up not far from the site of the monastery, I once set out with a school friend determined to check on the accuracy of the guidebooks. Sifting sand was a tedious business but the contents of my wooden box demonstrate that our efforts were rewarded. Perhaps we should have reburied our finds or taken them to a local museum but at that time, such thoughts did not occur to us.

When eventually I left Cornwall, it was difficult to abandon my box of bones because over the years, my imagination had been at work. The bones had become not just those of a Celtic monk but of a Celtic saint and therefore, holy relics! They served too as reminder of the county of my birth, of its beauty and wildness and of the saints who first preached the Christian faith in Cornwall, where I too had learned and practised it.

Secondly, the bones became a symbol of my Celtic origins, of the Cornish people and especially of my own family, past and present, and of the stability and security which is gained from roots so firmly established. Thirdly, these brittle bones enabled me to look to the future. They were a solemn reminder that life on this earth will come to an end and that one day, my mortal remains will rest in a box. Death, after all, is the only certainty in this life. The bones, however, also symbolized hope, for those who embrace the faith proclaimed by the Celtic saints believe that their lives are rooted not in Cornwall nor in any particular place on earth, but in Christ and that their true family is the family of God.

There is a famous scene in Shakespeare's *Hamlet* which vividly conveys that awareness of mortality which suddenly grips us when we gaze upon human bones. Hamlet shares his thoughts on the subject with his friend Horatio, as they watch a gravedigger throw a human skull to the surface:

> *That skull had a tongue in it, and could sing once' ... 'This might be the pate of a politician' ... 'Or of a courtier, which could say "Good morrow, sweet lord! How dost thou, sweet Lord?"'*
>
> *When the grave-digger throws up another skull, Hamlet continues: 'There's another. Why may not that be the skull of a lawyer? Where be his quiddits now, his quillits, his cases, his tenures, and his tricks?*

In contrast to these rather depressing thoughts of Hamlet, there is a passage in the Bible about a valley of dry bones which is full of hope. In a visionary experience, the prophet Ezekiel is assured that, just as God could cause breath to enter into the bones which surrounded the prophet, so God would give new life to the people of Israel after their long exile and they would return to their homeland and rebuild their lives (Ezekiel 37: 1-14).

Thus we see that dry crumbling bones need not speak to us only of death and despair but can speak also of new life and hope, and of the resurrection.

Thought Christian hope has been described as 'faith transferred to the future'. What do you think this means? Is it a good description?

Prayer Grant, O Risen Lord, that we may abound in hope and knowing your will, may faithfully perform it, empowered by your grace, O Lord of the dead and of the living. Amen.

Heaven

16. Heaven I: Like a City?
17. Heaven II: A Place of Understanding?
18. Heaven III: Free from Suffering?
19. A Ticket for Heaven I: Conditions of Entry
20. A Ticket for Heaven II: Accepting God's Terms

Heaven I: Like a City?

A little while ago in a series of talks about science and religion, a university professor likened the ways in which a physicist worked to the ways of a theologian. 'Scientists,' he said, 'like theologians, do not deal with certainties - only theories, and their theories, like those of theologians, are often based on personal experience.'

If it is acceptable for scientists to deal not only with certainties but also with theories, then it is equally acceptable for theologians to deal with theory, rather than certainty, in attempting to talk about heaven. And even if, like the physicist, we can't verify heaven's existence, then we can, like the physicist, reinforce the idea of what heaven might be like. But where do ideas about heaven come from? Here again, we find that the ideas of the theologian are based, like those of the physicist, on personal experience. Heaven, then, can be described only in terms of human experience.

One of the favourite theories about heaven is that it is like a city. This is an idea found in the Book of Revelation in the Bible and it is also an idea much loved by a famous medieval monk called Bernard of Cluny who wrote a hymn about the heavenly city ['Jerusalem the Golden']. Many other famous theologians and writers also developed this imagery of the heavenly city - St Paul, St Augustine, Dante, Milton, John Bunyan and T.S. Eliot. But why a city - like London or Bristol? If you are not a natural country dweller, you may find the idea very attractive but perhaps many of you who love country life are beginning to think that if heaven is like a city, it's not worth bothering about. But before you give up the struggle, we ought to consider why the image of the city was used so frequently to describe heaven.

First, it was because it was realized that heaven could never be a lonely place. We shall need other people in order to appreciate it and presumably, we shall really enjoy heaven only if we have others with whom to share it.

Secondly, a city in ancient times was always considered a symbol of safety. It had walls, it offered protection from wild beasts, and rest and security for the traveller. Surely, then, heaven too must be a safe, secure and welcoming place.

Thirdly, a city, unlike a tribal camp or even a village, would contain and recognize the necessity for all types of people from all sorts of backgrounds who, once settled within its wall as citizens, would benefit from the privileges of city life - provided, of course, they were prepared to accept their responsibilities and live peacefully with their neighbours.

The image of the city for heaven is then an appropriate one, but like all images or similes or metaphors, its use is limited. We cannot claim to have discovered the whole truth about heaven through our experience of city life, any more than a scientist can claim to have discovered the whole truth about his or her field of research as the result of an isolated experience, but that experience can at least provide a useful basis for his or her theories. Think, for example, of Archimedes and his bath water or of Newton and the apple.

Theologians may not be able to verify heaven's existence but at least they, like the scientists, can reinforce the idea with theories arising from their experiences of life in a city.

In the end, however, we must admit, like the university professor, that both the scientist and the theologian can only live, not with certainties, but by their faith and their beliefs.

Thought

'Tis well averred
A scientific faith's absurd.

ROBERT BROWNING

Do you agree or disagree with this statement?

Prayer

O Lord, help us to fashion our citizenship here on earth after the pattern of your eternal city in heaven through Jesus Christ our Lord. Amen.

17 Heaven II: A Place of Understanding?

Physicists, like theologians, do not deal with certainties, only with theories, and physicists, like theologians, can reinforce their theories only by developing them from personal experiences. One of the theologians' ideas about heaven is that it is like a city: safe, secure and welcoming. But what else can human experience teach of heaven?

There was once a school with a member of staff who was greatly respected by teachers and pupils alike for her scholarship, integrity and honesty - although her forthright manner could sometimes be disconcerting. She did not waste words and her grammar was impeccable. She was often critical of the way in which words were used and, as a result, many a school report had to be rewritten by her teaching colleagues. She taught Latin and Greek and, as well as speaking French and Italian fluently, she could read and translate Arabic. When she retired, she began to learn Hebrew, claiming that this was necessary because, you never know, Hebrew might be the language of heaven and it would be so disappointing not to be able to understand a word of what was being spoken. Shortly after her death, a friend remarked: 'No doubt, by this time, Winifred has discovered that Hebrew really is the language of heaven, so her efforts have been rewarded.'

I am quite sure that understanding what is going on in heaven will not be dependent on any language in particular but Christians believe that 'understanding' will be an important aspect of life in the heavenly city. St Paul certainly thought so and wrote in one of his letters: 'For now we see through a mirror dimly, but then, we shall see face to face. Now, I know in part but then, I shall understand fully, even as I have been understood.' But what will St Paul understand fully? We all know what great satisfaction a sudden understanding of a mathematical problem or a French grammatical construction can bring. Confusion disappears. 'The light has dawned,' we say, but heaven is not going to be concerned with such mundane problems, for there will be more important things for us to think about.

Peter Abelard, the medieval scholar, claimed that in heaven: 'God shall be all', so presumably we shall begin to understand a little more about God and, as God is not only all but 'in all', we shall probably begin to understand other people. Equally important though, and St Paul makes this clear, heaven is the place in which 'we are understood' - and that really is reassuring. It is unpleasant enough not to understand but it is even worse not to be understood. For example, you can feel utterly miserable in a country where no one can speak your language. You can also feel frustrated, alone and even rebellious when no one understands you as a person, but when someone does take the trouble to do so, you begin to gain confidence and to realize that you are special - even unique.

There was once a university chaplain to whom students, sometimes in groups or as individuals, went for help with their grievances or problems. He always listened to them patiently until he was absolutely certain that they had told him everything they wanted him to hear. Then he would bring the discussion to an end with these words: 'I understand. I really do understand and I'm sure that God understands too but there is no guarantee that everyone else will see your point of view.' Young people left his study feeling as if the problem had been at least partially resolved, simply because someone had taken the trouble to listen and to sympathize.

People like that priest, with a rare capacity for understanding others, can give us just a glimpse of heaven because they can show us, even in this life, what it is like to be uniquely known and understood and that is, of course, the way in which each of us is known and understood by God himself.

What brings about such understanding? Yet again we can turn to the Middle Ages for an answer, and this time to an explanation given by a monk called Aelred of Rievaulx, a monastery in Yorkshire. He was a delightful man and hundreds of monks joined his community. It was such a happy monastery that he liked to think of it as a reflection of heaven on earth. 'The source of all human understanding is God,' Aelred wrote, 'and since God is all and in all, in heaven, our human love gives way to divine compassion and we become of one heart and mind, and our understanding of each other is complete for, in God, we shall know as we are known.'

Prayer

O Divine Master, grant that I may not so much seek
to be consoled, as to console;
to be understood, as to understand;
to be loved, as to love.

PART OF A WELL-KNOWN PRAYER OF ST FRANCIS OF ASSISI

Heaven III: Free from Suffering?

The theologian can base his or her ideas about heaven only on human experiences - but not all human experiences are pleasant, some are extremely painful. So how can these speak to us of heaven?

It is only after we have lived through a period of suffering that we can really appreciate just how pleasant and satisfying normal life can be because, usually, we take so much for granted. There are however few people who can go through the whole of their lives without having to endure pain or difficulties of some kind. I don't mean putting up with minor ailments or inconveniences but with real suffering caused by physical disabilities like blindness, deafness or by being confined to a wheelchair. Not all suffering is physical, though, and some people endure bouts of severe depression or are forced to face up to the consequences of tragic accidents. There are those too who live in a state of total frustration - some because they suffer from constant pressure of work and others because they are unable to find employment. Suffering can also result from personality problems like acute shyness or the inability to relate to others. In today's society, especially, family problems, homelessness and poverty are common causes of suffering and so often we are totally unaware of the pain which many people endure or we consciously ignore it. Yet all these experiences can help us to see what heaven is like, for one aspect of heaven is to be released from suffering of whatever kind it happens to be.

A person who wrote and taught a great deal about heaven as a result of his own suffering was the famous medieval scholar Peter Abelard. The difficulties he had to face during his life gave him a deep spiritual insight into what he thought we should expect of heaven.

The tragic story of Peter Abelard and Heloise is almost as well known as that of Romeo and Juliet - but Abelard and Heloise were real people and their story is known through the letters they exchanged. They had to live their lives separated from each other. 'All that is left for us in this life is suffering, as great as our love has been,' wrote Heloise. They accepted their situation with great courage and looked forward to the new and different relationship they would experience in heaven - for they believed that 'in heaven they would neither marry nor be given in marriage'. 'Thou, O God,' prayed Abelard, 'hast parted us, when and in what manner it pleased thee. What thou hast parted for a time on earth, unite for ever to thyself in heaven.'

It was not only the frustration and sadness of the separation from Heloise which Abelard had to endure but he also had to contend with other very serious difficulties. As a leading scholar, he seemed to find himself in constant conflict with other scholars of his day. Abelard was a man of principle and argued for what he believed to be the truth, even though he was accused of heresy.

These fierce controversies also coloured his image of heaven and, in a famous hymn, he expressed his thoughts. For him, heaven is:

where trust is upheld
where there is peace and no conflict
where all friendships and relationships are hallowed in Christ
where wish and fulfilment are one
where all that is prayed for is granted
where there are no troubles, no distractions, no dangers
but only everlasting praise is offered 'to God who is all and in all.'

Thought How does Abelard's description of 'heaven' compare with any ideas you might have on the subject? To what extent are your thoughts coloured by your own experiences?

Prayer Merciful God, our heavenly Father, we bring before you all those who are sick in body, mind or spirit. Give them comfort in their pain and distress and bless those who work to relieve their pain and suffering through Jesus Christ our Lord. Amen.

19 A Ticket for Heaven I: Conditions of Entry

People who are committed to a religious faith, and often those who are not, have a variety of theories about heaven. One aspect of the subject is how you qualify for entry.

You cannot apply for a ticket just as you might for a football match or major pop concert – although surprisingly, the process of seeking a place in heaven is similar, in just one way, to acquiring entry for such events. For example, when you send for a ticket for Wimbledon or the Cup Final, you cannot be sure that your application will be successful. All you can do is to wait and to hope. The decision does not rest with you but with the bureaucrats who issue the tickets. Similarly, you do not make the decision about your entry to heaven, that is for God to decide.

Is there nothing then that we can do to persuade the Almighty that we are worthy, nothing that we can do to convince him that we merit such a reward? Could we perhaps earn our entry by acquiring appropriate qualifications, just as one qualifies for a place at university by gaining good academic results in the required subjects? Surely, if we attend religious services regularly and undertake sponsored swims or walks for charity or visit the sick and the elderly, we would deserve to be rewarded. St Paul, however, in a letter to the early Christians in Rome, makes it quite clear that 'good works' will not guarantee an easy entry to heaven.

Maybe, then, a place could be assured to us if our parents or godparents were good and godly people, who prayed hard for us on a daily basis. That, perhaps, would enable us to inherit the right of entry because with our names constantly mentioned in their prayers, God would not lose sight of us.

That you could inherit a place in heaven was certainly the view of some religious groups amongst the Jews in the time of Jesus, a view that he contradicted on more than one occasion.

So if there are no tickets, no way of earning entry, no inherited rights, how does one gain a place in heaven? According to the teaching of Jesus, particularly in the parables, entry depends entirely on an invitation, a gracious invitation from God himself. It is not like an invitation to a Royal Garden Party, highly selective and issued only to the great and the good, who represent a particular organization or who have served the community well. God's invitations are issued freely and widely, sometimes to the most unexpected people. Even, however, receiving an invitation does not guarantee success because it is the way in which people respond which is all important. Jesus himself admitted this, when he said: 'Many are called but few are chosen.'

The invitation is always issued on God's terms and it is whether or not these terms can be complied with that is really significant.

The conditions of entry are not related to what we do or what we have achieved. What really matters is the sort of people we are, and the quality which is required above all else is humility. There is no doubt that this is most clearly apparent in our lives from our attitude to others. Jesus demonstrated what is meant by humility through his symbolic actions at the last supper he shared with his friends, when: 'He poured water into a basin and began to wash the disciples' feet and wipe them with a towel ... "If I then, your Lord and teacher, have washed your feet, you also ought to wash one another's feet. For I have given you an example that you also should do as I have done to you."'

On another occasion, the ambitious mother of two of his disciples asked if her sons, James and John, could sit one at his right hand and the other at his left, in his kingdom. Jesus replied that she did not really understand what she was asking. He then addressed his disciples in these words: 'Whoever would be great among you must be your servant, and whoever would be first among you, must be slave of all.'

Thought Jesus once said: 'For everyone who exalts himself will be humbled and he who humbles himself will be exalted.'

What do you think he meant by this?

Prayer O Lord Jesus, teach us to put others before ourselves and to serve you in true humility. Amen.

Charles Williams was a mid-twentieth-century poet and novelist. He was one of an influential group of writers, two of whom are well known because they wrote popular children's books. One was J.R.R. Tolkien, the author of *The Hobbit*, and another, C.S. Lewis, who wrote the Narnia books. Many of you will also be aware that the stories of both these writers have deeper meanings than at first appear. Charles Williams also wrote novels and poems which when thought about seriously, convey deep and significant truths. One of his poems was an original and fascinating version of a parable which Jesus told about a wedding feast a king gave for his son. Many of the guests who were invited turned down the invitation at the last minute. Amongst those who did accept was a man who refused to wear the wedding garment which had been requested by his host for this special occasion. As a result, the king ordered his attendants to 'cast him into the outer darkness'. Thus Jesus demonstrated that we can enter the kingdom of heaven only on God's terms.

In Charles Williams' version of the parable, the king became 'The Prince Immanuel' and he hosted not a feast but a ball. Invitations were issued stating quite clearly that the guests must wear 'Fancy Dress'. On this occasion however, as you will learn from the poem, 'Fancy Dress' meant not merely wearing someone else's clothes but also recognizing and displaying the good qualities of the person represented by the distinctive style of dress.

One minor lord of the realm was so conscious of his own importance and so satisfied with his position in life, that he lacked the humility to comply with the Prince's requirements. Thus entry to the ball was refused to him and in this version, he was politely escorted to his car. However, the lesson to be learnt from Charles Williams' version of the parable is identical to that of the biblical account: we can be accepted by God only on his conditions and not on our own.

[**Note** This poem lends itself to dramatization.]

Apologue on the Parable of the Wedding Garment

The Prince Immanuel gave a ball:
cards, adequately sent to all
who by the smallest kind of claim
were known to royalty by name,
held, red on white, the neat express
instruction printed: Fancy Dress.
Within Earth's town there chanced to be
a gentleman of quality
whose table, delicately decked,

centred at times the Court's elect;
there Under - Secretaries dined,
Gold Sticks in Waiting spoke their mind,
or through the smoke of their cigars
discussed the taxes and the wars,
and ran administrations down,
but always blessed the Triune Crown.

The ball drew near; the evening came.
Our lordling, conscious of his name,
retained particular distaste
for dressing-up, and half-effaced,
by subjective sleight of eye
objectionable objectivity—
the card's direction. 'I long since
have been familiar with the Prince
at public meetings and bazaars,
and even ridden in his cars,'
he thought; 'his Highness will excuse
a freedom, knowing that I use
always my motto to obey:
Egomet semper: I alway.'

Neatly and shiningly achieved
in evening dress, his car received
his figure, masked but otherwise
completely in his usual guise.
Behold, the Palace; and the guest
Approached the Door among the rest.

The Great Hall opened: at his side
a voice breathed: 'Pardon, sir.' He spied,
half turned, a footman. 'Sir, your card—
dare I request? This Door is barred
to all if not in fancy dress.'
'Nonsense.' 'Your card, sir!' 'I confess
I have not strictly … an old friend …
his Highness … come, let me ascend.

My family has always been
in its own exquisite habit seen.
What, argue?' Dropping rays of light
the footman uttered: 'Sir, tonight
is strictly kept as strictly given;
the fair equivalents of heaven
exhibit at our lord's desire
their other selves, and all require
virtues and beauties not their own
ere genuflecting at the Throne.

Sir, by your leave.' 'But—' 'Look and see.'
The footman's blazing livery
in half-withdrawal left the throng
clear to his eyes. He saw along
the Great Hall and the Heavenly Stair
one blaze of glorious changes there.
Cloaks, brooches, decorations, swords,
jewels—every virtue that affords
(by dispensation of the Throne)
beauty to wearers not their own.
This guest his brother's courage wore;
that, his wife's zeal, while, just before,
she in his steady patience shone;
there a young lover had put on
the fine integrity of sense
his mistress used; magnificence
a father borrowed of his son,
who was not there ashamed to don
his father's wise economy.
No he or she was he or she
merely: no single being dared,
except the Angels of the Guard,
come without other kind of dress
than his poor life had to profess,
and yet those very robes were shown,
when from preserval as his own
into another's glory given,
bright ambiguities of heaven.

Below each change was manifest:
above, the Prince received each guest,
smiling. Our lordling gazed; in vain
he at the footman glanced again.
He had his own; his own was all
But that permitted at the Ball.
The darkness creeping down the street
received his virtuous shining feet;
and, courteous as such beings are,
the Angels bowed him to his car.

CHARLES WILLIAMS

Thought Jesus said: 'Whoever does not receive the Kingdom of God like a child shall not enter it.'

Prayer Enable us, O God, to see the good in others, and to recognize the weaknesses in ourselves through Jesus Christ our Lord. Amen.

People

21 An Architect of the People

Some years ago in the Hayward Gallery, there was an exhibition of the work of Le Corbusier.

Le Corbusier was an early-twentieth-century architect and it has been said that a knowledge of his achievements is essential for an understanding of the architecture of the last hundred years.

Le Corbusier, however, was not only an architect. He was also a talented painter, a sculptor, a designer and a philosopher and every aspect of his work was displayed in the exhibition.

Le Corbusier once said of himself: 'I exist, I am a mathematician, a geometrician and I am religious – that is to say, I can believe in a Gigantic ideal which dominates me and which I can hope to achieve.' Perhaps it was because he believed in this 'Gigantic ideal' – something greater and outside himself – that he achieved so much.

Although he began his career as an architect designing houses in his native Switzerland, he went on to design public and private buildings, churches and urban schemes in five continents. The height of his achievement was his design for the capital city Chandigarh in the Punjab. Le Corbusier was also a talented artist and his paintings influenced Picasso. He was a man of ideas and his philosophy had a marked effect on both Freud, the psychoanalyst, and the writer James Joyce. So Le Corbusier really was a man of creative genius.

One of the most impressive things about him, however, was that he cared for ordinary people and believed passionately in giving each individual scope in which to develop his or her personality. This was why he was so interested in schemes and plans for urban centres and inner-city areas.

In his designs for houses and flats in urban areas, he surrounded his buildings with grass and trees so that people, though they lived in towns, would not be unaware of the beauty of nature. He did not want them to feel restricted and hedged-in. Even in the tall blocks of flats where space was limited, he wanted to ensure that everyone who lived there had somewhere to be himself – a space, no matter how small, which he could call his own. So Le Corbusier in his designs included alcoves in walls and deep window seats where children could play or hide. He made frequent use of partitions so that women could sew, read, write or knit in peace, cut off from the work and the kitchen areas, or where men could read their newspapers or pursue their hobbies without interruption. So much family friction, he realized, arose from the fact that often people had no corner, no space in which they could be themselves. Homes, he believed, should be functional, fulfilling the needs of those who lived in them and not restricting their lifestyle.

Le Corbusier's buildings therefore reflected not just his amazing skill as a mathematician and geometrician but also his ideals - which sprang from his religious outlook on life. He believed that all men and women should be given the opportunity to develop their personalities and strive after their ideals, so that they, like Le Corbusier, could hope to achieve them - and in so doing become, as he said: 'the sort of people God intended them to be.'

Thought What would be your guiding principles and priorities if you were designing houses or flats for normal family use?

Prayer Almighty God, bless we beseech you our homes. Grant that your presence may dwell in them, enabling us to live with each other in harmony and peace. Give us true compassion so that we may be alive to the needs of the homeless, and bless our efforts to lighten the burdens of the poor and distressed through Jesus Christ our Lord. Amen.

The Saint Who Talked Too Much

Artists generally are not enthusiastic about painting portraits of children. The reason for this is that because a child's character has not been properly formed, the finished product might prove to be lacking in depth. An exhibition at the Royal Academy in 1999, however, demonstrated beyond all doubt that the artist Van Dyck, who was born in Antwerp in 1599, had no qualms in this respect because he was an exceptionally talented painter of children. He appeared to be in sympathy with them and was able to capture their engaging childishness and was happy, too, to include their pets in his paintings. As a small man physically, he did not literally 'look down' on children and this may have helped him to identify with them.

There is one child who, had she lived a couple of centuries later, would have been an excellent subject for a portrait by Van Dyck or by any other artist. This was because she exhibited from an early age the independence of mind and lively traits of character which she displayed until the end of her life. Like Mother Teresa of Calcutta, she identified with the suffering of the world at the time in which she lived. Her name was Catherine of Siena and she was born in the fourteenth century.

As a child, Catherine was strong willed, full of fun and uncontrollably talkative but quite religious. At the age of seven, she expressed a desire to be a nun but her father, who did not take her seriously, was determined to find her a suitable husband. Under the influence of her sister, Catherine forgot her early resolution for a while and started to enjoy life. We are told that she began to use 'make up' and dyed her hair the blonde colour which the Sienese men admired.

In 1362, her sister, who was by this time married, died in childbirth and Catherine was devastated. She immediately adopted a more serious lifestyle and vowed that she would, after all, become a nun. Her father, displeased with this decision, continued his search to find her a suitable and wealthy husband. Catherine, determined to offset his marriage plans, shaved off her hair. Her horrified family, in order to demonstrate what life was like for a woman who refused to marry and have a household of her own, insisted that she undertook all the domestic chores. Catherine did not complain and did all that was asked of her.

Eventually, she skilfully talked her father around to her point of view and at the age of eighteen, became a nun. Initially, she lived rather like a recluse, believing that she could serve God properly only by cutting herself off from the world. Then, quite suddenly, she changed her mind and concluded that she could learn to love God more effectively in the service of others. She gave up her solitude and began to minister to the needy, the sick and those whom no one else would touch, the lepers and those afflicted with plague. Wherever she turned, she said, she saw the face of Christ in the poor and the suffering.

Yet, for all her saintliness, she did not lose her lively disposition, nor did she ever learn to control her tendency to talk too much. It often happened, said one of her friends, that 'her flow of speech would keep running on and on ... and weighed down by sluggishness, I would slip off imperceptively into dreamland. Catherine would keep on talking and then, noting that I was asleep, would make a sudden noise to awaken me, adding with exasperation "I might as well be talking to the wall as to you about the things of God."'

Catherine's deep concern for others and for the things of God did not go unnoticed and she gradually emerged, like Mother Teresa, as a woman of love and peace and great authority. All ranks of people sought her advice, and medieval sources tell us that the grace and power of her presence reconciled divided and warring princes. Rulers sought her counsel and even the Pope asked for her help - her influence, like Mother Teresa's was worldwide.

If an artist had painted a portrait of St Catherine (as she later became known) as a child, there is no doubt that it would have reflected her delightful personality, her liveliness, her determination and religious commitment, characteristics which were obvious from her earliest years and which she retained to the end of her life - a life lived in the service of others.

Thought St Catherine said: 'Whenever I turn, I see the face of Christ in the poor and the suffering.'

Prayer O God, set our hearts at liberty from the service of ourselves, that we may live our lives in the service of others. Amen.

A Good Person

Susan Hill, in one of her novels, *Gentleman and Ladies*, describes what an enormous effect the presence at a funeral of a strange man in black boots, holding a bunch of stolen snowdrops, had upon the village of Haverstock and especially upon an elderly widow, Mrs Florence Ames. She tried to persuade Mr Gaily, the name of the man who had caused this disturbance, to meet one of her friends whom she described as 'a good person'. Mr Gaily, who was exceedingly shy and therefore reluctant to do so, asked: 'What is a good person?' In seeking a suitable definition, he was in fact asking a question which had exercised the minds of philosophers for hundreds of years.

The Greek philosopher Plato spent much of his life struggling with the problem and his book *The Republic* contains several attempts to explain what is meant by 'a good man'. 'A good man,' he wrote, 'is one who is not given to doing wrong', or 'a good man is one who never harms people, whether friends or enemies', or perhaps, 'a good man is one who does not study his own interests but is concerned with the interests of others, just as a good doctor is not primarily concerned with his own body but mainly with those of his patients', or, he writes, 'a good man is a man whose reason rules, who shows self-control and whose life reflects internal harmony'.

However, Plato eventually concluded that such perfection could be produced only by the perfect society, for people are not isolated individuals. A 'good man' therefore is the product of a good state.

Another philosopher, Justin Martyr, who lived in the second century A.D., reached rather different conclusions about 'a good man'. As a boy, Justin had an insatiable intellectual curiosity. He studied not only the philosophy of his own time but also the history of philosophy. He applied his mind to the ideas of the Stoics, he listened to the followers of Pythagoras and he read Plato's writings. In order to find solitude, he often sat in a field not far from the sea. He described in his own writings how, on one occasion, an old man interrupted his solitary meditations. 'He was looking,' Justin wrote 'for some members of his household, his grandchildren, when he noticed my glance fastened upon him. I explained that I was a philosopher and upon being told this, the elderly man began to ask me questions of a kind which old and wise men have a habit of placing before clever young philosophers. The gist of what he said was that one ounce of experimental knowledge of God was worth all the theorectical extravagance of the philosophers put together.'

Justin admitted that, when the old man had eventually defeated all his own philosophical certainties, he asked him where he should look for guidance. The man replied: 'There existed, long before this time, certain men more ancient than all those who are counted philosophers, men righteous and beloved of God, called prophets.' Justin then wrote: 'A flame was kindled in my mind,' and he went on to tell how he read and was filled with a love for those biblical prophets and for those who were the friends of Jesus. Thus it was, he claimed: 'I became the true philosopher' and for Justin, the question about 'a good man' was solved. 'If you have any self-respect, if you are looking eagerly for salvation, if you believe in God, it is open to you or to anyone else to meet the Christ of God, that after initiation [by this he meant baptism], you too may live a truly good and happy life'. Thus for Justin, 'a good man' was a man who had met 'the Christ of God'.

Justin never gave up as a philosopher, for he taught Christianity as pure philosophy. He was always the intellectual and eventually suffered martyrdom for upholding his particular philosophy of 'the good man' - a man, he claimed, who 'upheld the true teaching' and held it in what he described as 'the true way'. Justin believed that 'a good man' was not good because he himself had managed to achieve inner peace but was one who, having been in touch with God, reflected God's goodness. Jesus himself had acknowledged this when he claimed: 'No man is good, save God.'

Thought

Cardinal Hume, in his book *To be a Pilgrim,* wrote: 'If you become good and holy, it is because God made you so. You will not know it anyway, for a really good man is unaware of his goodness.'

Prayer

Heavenly Father, in whom we live and move and have our being, so guide and direct our lives with your Holy Spirit that others may see your divine love and goodness reflected in our lives through Jesus Christ our Lord. Amen.

Sinner and Saint

As a boy, I did not care for lessons and I disliked being forced to study. I would not have studied at all if I had not been forced to do so.

As a boy, I preferred adventure stories to more valuable studies and I wasted my brains on foolish delusions.

Many and many a time, I lied to my masters and my parents and deceived them because I wanted to play games or to watch some futile show. ... I was willing to steal and steal I did, although it was not because I was lacking in anything nor because I wanted to enjoy the things I coveted stealing. It was the theft itself which I enjoyed.

There was a pear tree near our garden and, late one night, a band of ruffians, myself included, stripped the pear tree of fruit and took the enormous quantity of pears, not to eat them ourselves but simply to throw them to the pigs. We may have eaten some of the pears but the real pleasure consisted in doing something that was forbidden.

An act of vandalism we would say - but who is this who writes so openly about his misspent youth? Were these quotations extracted from an article by a well-known criminal or are they from the opening chapters of the autobiography of an infamous rogue? The quotations are, in fact, from the writings of one of the world's greatest saints - St Augustine of Hippo, born in 354 A.D.

His life has always had a special appeal because he was a great sinner who became a great saint; and greatness is all the more admirable if it is achieved against the odds.

St Augustine paints so black a picture of his past that the reader may easily lose sight of the good qualities which he possessed. He was, for example, according to his mother, a very affectionate son - as naughty children often are!

When St Augustine wrote the book from which I have been quoting, he already had a considerable reputation for his saintliness and one of the reasons why he wrote was to persuade his admirers that any good qualities he possessed were his only by the grace of God.

St Augustine, although he did not enjoy his studies as a schoolboy, was a young man of considerable intellect and a thinker, who was genuinely interested in philosophy. In his questioning about the origin of the world and his genuine search for the truth, he adopted some rather weird ideas and for a while led a rather 'hippie' type of existence. When he was in his late teens, his mother was in despair about her son, whose life seemed to be without purpose or direction, given over to indulgence and what seemed to her, utter and complete idleness.

She asked a wise man to speak seriously to Augustine in the hope that he would bring him to his senses. The wise man, however, refused and explained that Augustine was not ready for such advice because he was 'brimming over' with the novelty of strange ideas. 'Leave him alone,' he said. 'Just pray for him. From his own reading he will eventually discover his mistakes and be led to a philosophy of life which will prove satisfying.'

Augustine eventually qualified as a teacher of rhetoric and, after lecturing for a while in North Africa, moved to Rome, not for the sake of his career but because he believed it would be easier to teach there. He wrote: 'The behaviour of the students at Rome was quieter. Discipline was stricter and they were not permitted to rush as they pleased into the lecture rooms. In fact, they were not admitted at all without their master's permission.' 'In Carthage,' he commented, 'the young students are beyond control and they come into lecture rooms like a troop of maniacs.' Augustine, once himself an undisciplined student, was now obliged to endure the lack of self-control in others.

All through these years as a teacher, he continued in his quest for a satisfactory philosophy of life and finally found it in the teaching of a Christian philosopher called Ambrose. Once converted to Christianity, Augustine was ordained and later consecrated Bishop. He was soon recognized as one of the most important and influential theologians and teachers in the history of the Church. His best-known writing, *The Confessions of Saint Augustine*, contains not so much the confession of his sins as the confession of his faith – the faith which he himself had ultimately discovered after a long and agonizing search, which he summed up in the words of a famous prayer: 'You made us, O God, for yourself and our hearts are restless till they rest in thee.'

Prayer

O God, in whom all things live,
You command us to seek you
And you are ready to be found.
To know you is life,
To serve you is freedom,
To praise you is joy. Amen.

25 Salvador Dalí I: 'The Hybercubic Body'

Drawing based on 'The Hypercubic Body', 1954, reproduced in *Dalí* by Luis Romero (Chartwell Books Inc., 1975).

After Picasso, Salvador Dalí is probably the most universally famous twentieth-century painter. He was born in Catalonia in northern Spain and the Surrealist style of art is virtually defined by his work, although he was never wholly accepted by the Surrealists.

Who were the Surrealists and what were they trying to achieve? In the 1920s, when psycho-analysis was a very new science, it opened up interesting subject matter for painters. The Surrealists were artists who seized upon this and attempted to tap the creative and imaginative forces of the mind in the unconscious. Consequently, their work is full of strange imagery, which is sometimes grotesque and often disturbing - as many of Dalí's paintings are.

Dalí, however, had an unusual appetite for new ideas and painted in a number of different styles, from Cubism to Pop Art. Towards the end of his career, although not religious in the way most people would understand it, he made frequent use of Christian devotional subjects. Consequently, much of his later work was strongly influenced by the traditions and symbolism of Catholic Spain and far from Surrealism in spirit.

One such painting, which he calls 'The Hypercubic Body', depicts the crucifixion of Jesus, a subject which throughout the last two millennia has constantly appealed to artists of the Western World. In Dalí's painting, the cross is a very solid and powerful object formed from seven cubes, three of which are black and four of which are gold. The contrasting colours remind the spectator that for Jesus, the crucifixion was the moment of both his humiliation and his triumph.

The cubic cross is suspended above an empty chess-board. It is as if a game has just finished and in a sense, you could say that it had because in the Gospels, we read that the disciples who had followed Jesus had forsaken him and fled. To those who watched the crucifixion from afar, or even at the foot of the cross, it must have seemed as if this was the end of the story of Jesus of Nazareth. Those who had put their trust in his message did not see any hope in the future. Yet, in the painting, because the chess-board, although empty, is still open, it could indicate that it stands ready for another game to begin, which of course it did, with the resurrection. Those who had originally joined in 'the game' or mission of Jesus, regained their faith and continued his work, once they were convinced that he had risen from the dead.

A black sky forms the background to the cross and the light of the sun can only just be seen behind the distant landscape - a visible reminder of what the Gospel writers describe as 'darkness over all the land from the sixth until the ninth hour'. Yet, in Dalí's painting, a light shines on the cross, not from the sun, but from the opposite direction, and highlights the figure of Jesus. It is as if God's power, like the light of the sun, has been temporarily withdrawn from the world in order to concentrate on the action which is taking place on the cross.

Jesus' body is held to the cross, not by nails, but by three small cubes which appear almost magnetic. This suggests that, had he chosen to do so, by the movement of an arm or leg, he could have released himself. It recalls the taunt of the passers-by: 'If you are the Son of God, come down from the cross.' Jesus had resisted a similar temptation in the wilderness, early in his ministry, by his refusal to perform some spectacular feat in order to prove that he was the Son of God.

In Dalí's painting, Jesus is not depicted as weak and exhausted but as young and vigorous, with his head held high - a reminder, perhaps, of a saying of St Paul: that the word of the cross 'to those who are being saved is the power of God'.

In the left-hand corner of the painting, on a platform, stands a dignified woman dressed in a white brocade, rather like a coronation robe. Flung over her shoulder is a length of golden cloth, presumably ready to wrap the body for the burial. The model for the woman was Dalí's wife, Gala, who in this painting represents Mary, the mother of Jesus. Her eyes are riveted on her son and the light from the cross reflects upon her face. Although she is majestic and dignified and beautifully painted by the artist, the spectator, by following her gaze, is forced to look once more at the cubic cross and to ponder upon its meaning.

Prayer

Make known, O Lord, to those who doubt the way of truth and peace, and lead them to see your glory revealed in the person of your son, Jesus Christ our Lord. Amen.

Thought

Although Dalí painted religious subjects, he once admitted that with regard to God, his attitude was the same as Voltaire's. Then he related this anecdote:

> *The philosopher was walking along a street with a friend one day, when they saw a priest on his way to someone's sick bed with the Blessed Sacrament. Voltaire took off his hat, at which his friend asked why he showed such respect, given his standpoint regarding the Church and religion. Voltaire replied, 'God and I always greet each other, even though we never speak'.*

On another occasion when asked: 'Do you believe in God?', Dalí replied: 'Based on my reason and based on what the latest scientific discoveries of our times have shown me, I am convinced that God exists.'

Salvador Dalí II: 'The Dream of Christopher Columbus'

Drawing based on 'The Dream of Christopher Columbus', 1958, reproduced in *Dalí* by Luis Romero (Chartwell Books Inc., 1975).

'The Dream of Christopher Columbus' may not at first appear to be the subject for a religious picture but after one glance at Dalí's painting, there is no doubt that this was how he interpreted it. He used his imagination to depict the voyages of Christopher Columbus in the context of the fifteenth century. At that time, it was thought that the discovery of lands beyond the Atlantic would bring a new spiritual empire to the Church and a field for missionary activity. The voyages, therefore, were not merely a quest for spice and gold because religious aspirations were blended with a desire for financial gain.

The Portuguese had already found one way to India by sailing to the east but many believed that there was another way to the west, across the Atlantic. It was an idea inspired by legend, which told of a floating island called Atlantis. It was said that many years ago, several bishops and their congregations had fled there to escape from the attacks of the barbarians. Christopher Columbus claimed that from the age of twenty-eight, he longed to discover both the descendants of these Christians and the new route to Asia.

In order to achieve his ambition, he first sought the backing of the King of Portugal but when that was refused, he turned to Spain. A Spanish Commission considered his project for five years and then, much to his disappointment, rejected it. Eventually, however, through the influence of a priest and a woman high in the favour of Queen Isabella of Spain, he achieved the Queen's support. She was a deeply religious woman and he persuaded her to allow him to look for the 'lost' Christians. In 1492, she ordered him to take three ships and 'discover and acquire islands and mainland in the ocean sea', so Columbus pursued his dream.

Throughout the voyage, the fact that this was a religious quest was not forgotten. At half-hourly intervals, a boy who stood near the helmsman sang appropriate chants. At dawn for example, the sailors heard:

Blessed be the light of day
And the holy cross we say.

On reaching land, Columbus knelt down and thanked God and named the island which he had discovered 'San Salvador', which means 'Holy Saviour'. Although Christopher Columbus did not realize it, 'the islands and the mainland in the ocean sea' beyond, upon which he had stumbled, were an unknown continent, the new world, the Americas.

All this has been incorporated into Dalí's painting, for in it Columbus leaps ashore bearing in his right hand the banner of Santa Maria, the name of his ship. The figure on the banner is recognizable, for it is a portrayal of Dalí's wife, Gala, who in so many of his paintings is his model for Mary, the mother of Jesus. With his left hand, Columbus drags a rope to which is attached a heavy, black, iron crucifix, rather like an anchor, and behind him are the sails of his ship, decorated with huge gold crosses. In procession following Columbus are his sailors, some carrying tall wooden crosses, as if made from ships' masts, others bearing the multi-coloured flags of the provinces of Spain. Beyond them, the sea mingles with the sky and what appears to be a 'heavenly host' emerges in the distance. There is no doubt in this picture that the new world is being claimed for Christ.

That the painting depicts 'the dream' of Columbus, rather than the actual event, is made quite clear to us by Dalí. He includes in the picture the figure of a bishop (presumably one of the lost bishops) clutching his pastoral staff and raising his hand in blessing as the expedition lands, but historical records tell us that the arrival of Columbus was in fact watched 'by a group of native men on the beach' - hardly a spectacular welcome!

However, there is no doubt that, even if the lost Christians were not found, a new continent had been discovered and, in the fifteenth century, this in itself would have had an important religious significance.

Thought

What difference would it make if all new discoveries, not just geographical but scientific ones too, were seen in the context of the extension of God's Kingdom?

On a visit to Paris, Pope John Paul II concluded an address with these words: 'Marvellous scientific results have been achieved for the benefit of mankind but too often, science has been used towards ends which have destroyed human dignity.'

Prayer

Almighty God, guide and prosper all those who are devoted to scientific study and research, and grant that their discoveries may be used to the benefit of your world through Jesus Christ our Lord. Amen.

Two Strange Ladies I: Margery Kempe

The unique story of Margery Kempe was reported in *The Times* on 27 December 1934 and her biography, published two years later, became one of the season's bestsellers. Margery was born in 1373 but until the twentieth century, she was unknown, so her name hit newspaper headlines five hundred years after her death. All this was the result of the discovery of an ancient manuscript containing her story.

The book caused tremendous excitement amongst scholars. Students of English were fascinated because it was said to be the first biography in the English tongue. Historians were delighted because it threw light on the medieval scene; psychiatrists felt that Margery with her eccentric behaviour would be a superb subject for psycho-analysis, and the medical world was interested because of descriptions of ancient methods of treatment for illnesses. Theologians too were anxious to find out what Margery's life revealed about the practice of religion at the beginning of the fifteenth century.

The daughter of John Brunhom, who was five times mayor of King's Lynn, she married John Kempe, a burgess of Lynn, and bore him fourteen children. The birth of her first child deepened her religious feelings, which at times she found difficult to control. The sight of a crucifix could move her to tears, not just silent tears, for her biographer writes 'wild outbursts of weeping would suddenly seep from her and sometimes, by the vehemence of her sobs, cries and screams, she frightened people.' Once, after weeping 'boisterously' in a church, she was arrested and accused of being a 'false deceiver of the people'. Margery's feelings, however, were genuine. She wept for her own sins and for the wrongdoings of others. One priest refused to have her in his congregation because of her 'violent' weeping.

At the age of forty-one, Margery desired to express her religious fervour by going on a pilgrimage. Most medieval pilgrims chose to go to one of three holy places - the Holy Land, Rome or Santiago de Compostela in Spain - but Margery opted to visit all three. Her husband gave her permission to carry out what she considered 'The Lord's Commands' and together they visited the Archbishop of Canterbury to receive his blessing. Her husband then returned to King's Lynn but Margery set off to the Holy Land.

Her religious fervour made her travelling companions embarrassed because they objected to her constant sobbing. When she visited the places connected with the life of Christ, her weeping became more violent than ever. Although a trial to others, Margery herself claimed that this strange behaviour was a gift from God. 'As for my crying, my sobbing and my weeping and my tears, you know, O Lord, what reproof I have to bear because of it but grant, O Lord, that others may be moved by it,' she prayed.

Margery, however, had more positive virtues. She was extremely tender-hearted and generous to the poor, sick and aged. In those who suffered, she saw the 'wounded' Christ and she gave help and comfort to anyone in need. Her emotional temperament also made her fearless and outspoken. Once she was brought for trial before the Archbishop of York for her uncontrolled weeping. In response to his accusation that she was 'a right wicked woman', she replied, 'I also hear it said that you are a wicked man. And if you be as wicked as men say, you will never go to heaven unless you amend your ways.' Apparently, the Archbishop then treated her with more consideration.

In spite of her outspokenness, Margery was the most humble of women, referring to herself as 'the creature' thus reflecting her sense of her own unworthiness.

The true meaning of religion is thus not simply morality but morality touched by emotion.

MATTHEW ARNOLD

Thought Do you consider 'emotion' a help or a hindrance to the cause of religion?

Prayer Help us, O Lord God, to relieve the needy and the destitute, to comfort the distressed and to see you in all who are poor and desolate. Through Jesus Christ our Lord. Amen.

Two Strange Ladies II: Christina of Markyate

Christina was a remarkable woman who lived in the reign of Henry II at Markyate, a village not far from Luton. As we do not know her surname, she is usually referred to as Christina of Markyate and in Britain, the ruins of a priory are the most solid evidence for her existence. There is, however, carefully preserved in a museum in Germany, a very beautiful manuscript which tells us something about Christina. Scholars call it the St Albans Psalter but as it records the dates of the deaths of Christina's father, mother, her brothers and her friends, it almost certainly belonged to her.

For further information about Christina, we have to rely upon an account of her life which was written by a contemporary monk of the Abbey of St Albans and then incorporated much later into a fourteenth-century manuscript. From this, we learn that Christina had vowed in early life to become a nun. Her parents, however, had other ideas and forced her to go through a marriage ceremony with a Guild merchant of Huntingdon, her home town. Christina, determined to keep her vow of chastity, ran away. As she was unable to enter a convent without her husband's consent, she eventually joined a group of hermits at Markyate. From them, as well as from the Abbot of St Albans Abbey, Christina received much kindness and support.

Her life was by no means easy or comfortable but for the young Christina, her problem was not the discomfort but her beauty. Her biographer tells us that whoever came into contact with her was 'inflamed by her beauty and attracted by her fascinating personality'. Even the priest who acted as her spiritual guide fell desperately in love with her and had to cease hearing her confessions.

As a hermit, Christina's life was largely devoted to prayer and frequently she experienced 'visions'. What, however, in medieval times would be regarded as 'visions', we would probably describe as 'insights' - insights into perfectly normal events which were given spiritual meanings. People flocked to Christina for counsel and advice and constantly asked for her prayers. We are also told she had the ability to discern what was going to happen in the future. Again, this was no miraculous power but it arose from Christina's keen observation of those who lived around her and of those who came to seek the benefit of her wisdom. Detached from their way of life, she heard everyone's problems, showed concern for their welfare and gave good advice. Thus she achieved a position as adviser, peacemaker, prophet and even healer.

After the death of her husband, she was free to join a religious community. The Archbishop of York tried to persuade her to become the mother superior of a convent in that city but she refused that offer, as well as that which came from a great religious house in France at Fontevrault. Christina was a humble woman, who preferred to live with a few nuns at the little priory at Markyate. It was from there that she served the surrounding community and it was from there that her power and influence spread so widely.

Christina put herself into the position of becoming what today we would call an 'outsider'. By cutting herself off from the world, she was better able to serve the world and to be aware of the problems of others, than if she had lived a normal life within it.This is true to some extent of all saintly people. As a result of their detachment from worldly and material things, they can see more clearly how to transform people's lives. Those of us, on the other hand, who are falling over backwards to get involved and to conform to the standards of this world are incapable of transforming it.

St Paul wrote in his letter to the Romans:

Adapt yourselves no longer to the pattern of this present world, but let your minds be remade and your nature thus transformed. Then, you will be able to discern the will of God, and to know what is good, acceptable and perfect.

ROMANS 12:2

Thought Can you think of ways in which the world needs to be 'transformed'?

Prayer Grant, O Lord, that we may obediently reject the illusions of things temporal, and walk without faltering in the light of things eternal through Jesus Christ our Lord. Amen.

St Benedict and His Rule I: Leadership Qualities

Not so long ago, there was a brief news item in the national press about a group of management consultants, who were attending a conference to study a set of instructions which had originally been written in the sixth century for a group of monks. It seemed an unlikely story but you may be surprised to learn that this was not a pointless exercise.

The 'Rule of St Benedict', as these instructions or rules are commonly known, has had an enormous influence on western civilization and particularly on institutions like schools, colleges and hospitals. It is also important because it lays down the basic principles of any community life and shows a superb understanding of human nature. It is therefore just as relevant to those who are concerned with modern management as it was in the sixth century because the problems of community life are universal and timeless, and human nature does not change.

But who was St Benedict and what was his Rule? The facts about the Saint's life are not easy to establish because the only information we have about him was not written down until fifty years after his death. By that time, many legends had grown up about him and his biographer, Pope Gregory the Great, had difficulty in disentangling the truth from legendary accretion. However, we must be grateful for his efforts because without them, we should know nothing of St Benedict - only his name.

It seems that he was born in 480 A.D. at Nursia in Italy and educated in Rome at the time when the Roman Empire was in rapid decline. St Benedict, who had little patience with the undisciplined, immoral and greedy lifestyle of Roman society of his day, withdrew to live as a hermit in the hills beyond Rome. Gradually, others joined him and he established his first religious community. The idea caught on and soon there were several monasteries in that area. In 525, he founded the monastery at Monte Cassino, where he himself was Abbot for the rest of his life. It was here that he gave his monks the famous 'Rule', which helped them to live regular, disciplined lives. He called it his 'little rule for beginners'.

Within a short time, monasteries were established all over Europe and in England particularly, we owe a tremendous debt to the Benedictine monks. A group of them came, under St Augustine, in 597 to convert the English to the Christian faith and the first Benedictine monastery was established, with the permission of King Ethelbert, in Canterbury.

It is well known that in the Middle Ages, the monasteries were a civilizing influence on society. They were the centres of learning, where manuscripts were written and art and music flourished. They also acted as hospitals and charitable institutions for the sick and the poor. That we have few facts about the events in the life of St Benedict matters little, for in order to find out about an influential and remarkable person, it is important to study his character. In this respect, we are fortunate because we can learn so much about St Benedict from his Rule. At the outset, he states clearly that he hopes to order 'nothing harsh or rigorous', and the instructions he gives to his monks certainly reflect a gentle personality. For example, he knew that the younger ones especially, like most young people, found it difficult to get up early and so he writes:

> *The younger brethren shall have their beds in dormitories mixed with seniors ... Let them gently encourage one another on account of the excuses to which the sleepy are addicted.*

Learning that his monks, when it was their turn to serve meals, would suffer pangs of hunger, he writes:

> *Let the weekly servers, an hour before the meal, receive each of them over and above the regular allowance, a drink and some bread, in order that at the meal time, they may serve the brethren without murmuring and undue hardship.*

St Benedict also showed great compassion for the elderly and for the young boys growing up in the monastery:

> *Let the old men and the children be provided for by the authority of the Rule and on no account let the rigour of the Rule in regard to food be applied to them. Let them, on the contrary, receive compassionate consideration and take their meals before the regular hour.*

Benedict may have been gentle and kind but he was no 'soft touch'. He insisted on punctuality for the services in the monastery chapel:

> *Let the brethren abandon what they have in hand and assemble with the greatest speed, yet soberly.*

He was firm about accuracy and precision and any monk who read carelessly in the chapel was punished. Above all, he hated idleness: 'Idleness is the enemy of the soul.'

The clearest picture we have of St Benedict himself is in the advice he gives to the abbots who were in charge of the monasteries. The leadership qualities which he expected to find in them are those which we would hope to find in anyone in a position of authority in a modern community or institution - headteachers, college principals, chief executives of a company or business - and also in parents:

Let the abbot …
always set mercy above judgment …
hate ill doing but love the brethren; …
in administering correction, act with prudent moderation.
Let him always distrust his own frailty.
Let him study to be loved rather than feared.
Let him not be turbulent or anxious, overbearing or obstinate, jealous or too suspicious.
Let him be prudent and considerate in all his demands.

Let us hope that the management consultants who were studying the 'Rule' passed this wise advice on to those who were training to be managers.

Thought Above all, St Benedict believed in exercising 'compassionate consideration'. How would you explain this idea?

Prayer Guide, we beseech you, O Lord, the hearts and minds of those who hold positions of responsibility. Give them the vision of your truth and justice, and grant that, ever mindful of your holy will, they may look to the good of all those who are subject to their authority through Jesus Christ our Lord. Amen.

St Benedict and His Rule II: Living in Harmony

The Rule of St Benedict not only provides wise advice for those who are teaching others to develop management skills, but family life too could be greatly improved by putting some of his words of wisdom into practice. This is because St Benedict saw his communities as family groups with the abbot assuming a role of a parent, and the monks that of his children. People would certainly be better parents if they, like the abbots, acted with prudent moderation, studied to be loved rather than feared and avoided being turbulent, anxious, overbearing or obstinate.

But what of the monks? In what ways does St Benedict's advice to them bear any relevance to the behaviour which is expected of members of a community, or even of children in any family in the third millennium? You will, I think, be quite surprised by the familiar ring of some of these instructions to his monks.

> *They must not love too much speaking and when they speak, they must do so gently and seriously in a few and sensible words and they must not shout.*

> *If anyone loses or breaks anything in the kitchen or in the pantry, the dining-room, the garden or anywhere else, it must be reported at once.*

There is nothing more disruptive to family life than a child who is totally self-centred, attention seeking and constantly disobedient. Just as parents want their children to be co-operative members of the family, so St Benedict desired co-operation and obedience on the part of his monks: 'Let none follow what is good for himself but rather what is good for another.'

He wanted his monasteries to be stable and harmonious communities. He realized that this could result only by insisting on stability in the lives of his monks. So, once a monk had taken his vows, he was expected to remain within the same monastery. He was not allowed to move to another community just because he disliked the abbot or did not get on with the other monks. All the monks had to learn how important it was to live with each other in harmony. This again is true of any community. We do not choose our fellow students nor our lecturers and teachers and in an office, we have to work with colleagues even if we dislike them. Certainly in family life, we have no choice and have to accept our parents and our brothers and sisters and to learn to live with them.

As in all communities, St Benedict knew that there would be tensions and clashes of personality and so he warned his monks:

not to yield to anger
not to nurse a grudge
not to hold guile in one's heart
not to make a feigned peace
not to turn away from anyone who needs your love.

This is wise advice which everyone who lives with others would do well to heed if harmony is to be achieved.

The monks inevitably found certain aspects of monastic life difficult and limiting. This is an experience which is not unknown to students of any educational institution or to the employees of a large company, and even to the younger members of a family. There will always be restrictions in community life or difficulties with which we have to contend - a boring routine or timetable, insufficient books in a library, unattractive buildings and at home, household chores. St Benedict realized that at times, it was essential to practise perseverance and endurance; but he also knew that it was inadvisable to be constantly moving around, just because certain conditions of the community in which you lived did not meet with your approval. He encouraged his monks to face up to such irritations, difficulties and restrictions: 'Saying nothing, holding fast in patience, enduring all without growing weary or giving up.'

St Benedict, in his wisdom, knew that the creation of a harmonious and stable monastery depended upon the goodwill of every monk as well as the skill of the abbot. Likewise, in any community, demands are placed on every single member but the greatest responsibility rests with the leader, who must show 'compassionate consideration' to everyone under his or her authority. All this goes to show that the management consultants who met to study the Rule of St Benedict surely did not meet in vain.

Thought What restrictions do you find annoying or difficult? Do you think that St Benedict's advice is sound?

Prayer You, O Lord, gave us the commandment that we should love one another; give us also the grace that we may fulfil it. Grant that we may look to the good of others in word and deed and so live together in peace and harmony. Amen.

St Benedict and His Rule III: Moderation in All Things

Business Studies and Business Management are two of the most popular university courses these days, and I imagine that one of the first lessons to be learnt about running a successful business is the importance of efficiency. The principles of order and balance which help to produce an efficient institution run right through the organization of the monasteries of St Benedict.

Everything most be done at the proper time.
Everyone is to keep his proper place.

states the Benedictine Rule.

The pursuit of holiness, which was an important factor in the Rule, was not an excuse for muddle in the life of a monk, nor was devotion an acceptable reason for escaping from work. St Benedict wanted his monks to be balanced personalities and this, he knew, could be achieved only by helping them to lead the ordered existence of a life which followed a definite pattern. Each day they had to give time to worship, to study and to manual work.

He also believed in moderation. For example, individual monks were not expected to work so hard that they damaged their health and undermined their strength to a point that, in management circles, is known as 'burn out'. He gives in his Rule a wonderful description of someone suffering from this condition. Under stress as a result of overwork, a monk, he observes, becomes: 'excitable, anxious, overbearing, obstinate, jealous, oversuspicious and never able to stop.' Such a man, writes St Benedict, 'is never at rest'. He also knew that anyone living at this pace was a danger to the community because he could impose similar pressures on those amongst whom he lived. One of the abbot's duties was to prevent his monks from following this kind of existence. 'If they drive their flocks too hard, they will all die in a single day,' concludes St Benedict.

The Rule therefore sets out a careful rhythm of a monk's day in great detail, so that sufficient time is given to each of the monastery's three main activities.

Another important principle of the Rule is moderation. No one is expected to undertake the impossible:

If a brother is commanded to do what he considers impossible, let him receive the command but if he sees the weight of the burden altogether exceeds the measure of his strength, let him explain the reasons why he is unable to perform the task to his abbot calmly and at the right moment, without obstinacy and contentiousness.

St Benedict was certainly ahead of his time in making this point. For it is only comparatively recently that the secular world has recognized the importance of a system which allows employees the right to receive a just hearing when they wish to register a complaint.

Furthermore, St Benedict's principle of moderation is reflected in his appreciation of the difficult work which some of his monks had to undertake. For example, he realized that caring for the sick could be an extremely demanding task, and admitted that 'the brethren who are serving the sick are often provoked by unreasonable demands, yet they should be patiently borne with'.

Above all, the abbot of a monastery was expected to show compassion in adapting himself to the many dispositions of the brethren. Like any community, a monastery contained a variety of personalities, and it was important for the abbot to see them as individuals, and to recognize the needs and potential of each of his monks. From the Rule, we gather that the monasteries had many troublesome monks as well as the obedient, docile and patient ones. It was the duty of the abbot to humour, rebuke, persuade and encourage, thus adapting and accommodating himself to all in such a way that 'Like a good shepherd, he suffers no loss in the sheep committed to his care.'

St Benedict concludes his Rule with this sentence: 'The Rule is not meant to be a burden to you. It should help you to discover and to experience how great is the freedom to which you are called.' This again shows his deep understanding of human nature. He knew that people find freedom only by accepting themselves as they are, by doing the work they have to do, at this moment, in the places in which they happen to find themselves. The prize of freedom, according to St Benedict, is never gained by 'running away.'

Again, we turn to the management consultants and ask what they may have learnt from their study of the Rule of St Benedict. They would surely have admitted that the best communities or institutions are based on the principles of harmony, balance and moderation, where leaders value the importance of each individual; and where individuals each find freedom because they are aware of their own distinctive contribution to that community, and of the benefits they receive from the presence and co-operation of others.

Thought Benedictine monks and nuns claim that 'St Benedict, though dead, still speaks through his Rule.' What do you think they mean by this?

Prayer

Almighty God, give us wisdom to perceive you,
intellect to understand you, diligence to seek you,
patience to wait for you, vision to behold you,
a heart to meditate upon you, and life to proclaim you.
Amen.

If you have ever had a holiday in Cornwall, you may either have happy memories of fine golden sand, rugged cliffs, wild seas and clear rock pools, or even unhappy memories of interminable rainy days, narrow winding streets packed with summer visitors and of souvenir shops displaying Cornish piskies and every variety of lucky charm. A hundred and fifty years ago, Cornwall was not the popular tourist area that it is today but a wild, backward country rarely visited by outsiders and sparsely populated by poverty-stricken communities.

In 1834, a young man of thirty, with an impressive academic background, a scholarly interest in history and no mean poet, was appointed Vicar of the parish of Morwenstow, one of the most isolated parishes in the whole of England. Morwenstow is situated on the edge of the rugged cliffs of north Cornwall. In that part of the peninsula, the coast is pitiless and very few ships sailing near its cliffs have ever survived. The village church is built of grey granite and its pinnacled tower stands rock-like against the background of the ever restless sea.

When the new young Vicar, Robert Stephen Hawker, arrived at Morwenstow, he soon realized that he was undertaking a task as hard as the rocks which surrounded his parish. The parishioners, however, quickly came to the conclusion that, although their new parson seemed in so many ways a strange and eccentric character, he was tough enough to meet the challenge.

The parish was hardly what most of the clergy of his day would have regarded as a 'good living' – that is, financially well endowed. The vicarage was in ruins and partly used as a barn and the church building was ill cared for and surrounded by weeds and nettles.

The village had not had a resident priest for many years and the people were desperately in need of pastoral care. The farmers of the parish were simple and respectable folk. The rest of the inhabitants, after receiving wages in harvest time, eked out a precarious existence in the winter with smuggling or by watching eagerly for the shipwrecks that were certain to happen. The goods salvaged from the wrecks supplied them with the necessities of life. The planks provided firewood and the personal possessions of those who were drowned could be sold to provide extra comforts. In fact, the new incumbent soon discovered that the inhabitants of Morwenstow did not just wait for wrecks to take place, they sometimes caused them to happen. He noticed too that when a wreck was sighted, they would do nothing to help the drowning but obeyed what they claimed was an old Cornish proverb:

Save a stranger from the sea
And he will be your enemy.

In fact, in Morwenstow, a wreck was regarded as a gift from God.

Mr Hawker was horrified by the habits of his parishioners. He was determined to stop what seemed to him little better than cannibal behaviour but he had strange ways of reforming his flock. Always somewhat eccentric in style of dress, once he arrived at Morwenstow he decided to abandon the formal wear of a nineteenth-century clergyman and adapted his clothes to his surroundings. It is said that he wore a blue fisherman's sweater with a red cross. His coat was purple with black tails and his hat, pink and brimless. 'What is the point of a hat with a brim,' he said, 'when the wind rarely ceases blowing in Morwenstow? At least if a pink hat is blown off, it can easily be found.' Instead of shoes, he wore long fisherman's boots so that he was always at the ready to rush with his parishioners to the beach when there was a wreck. His aim, however, was very different from that of his flock.

When Mr Hawker reached the scene, his first task was not to grab the loot but to see if there were any survivors whom he could help or bodies which needed a reverent burial. Gradually, his parishioners began to learn from his example; that the saving of human life was more important than finding planks for firewood or filling their pockets with money and trinkets from the pouches of the survivors and the dead. This was not an easy lesson to teach in a village where many lived in extreme poverty. It was, however, the first lesson which Mr Hawker of Morwenstow instilled into the minds of his wayward flock.

Thought

The saving of human life is of far greater importance than the accumulation of material possessions.

This teaching is upheld by all the world's great religions. Yet even in the third millennium, human suffering and need are often ignored by those who could do so much to give relief. What more could be done to highlight the problem?

Prayer

O God, the Lord and giver of life, help us to uphold and to proclaim to the world that all human life is sacred. Guide and prosper the work of those engaged in medical research, and strengthen them with the assurance that they are fellow workers with you in their endeavours to find new ways of promoting health and healing through Jesus Christ our Lord. Amen.

The nineteenth-century Vicar of the remote village of Morwenstow, Robert Stephen Hawker, not only changed the attitude of his parishioners towards shipwrecks and those who survived them, he also instilled into his people how important it was to believe in the sanctity of human life. It was not long before they also learnt from his example that dead bodies too should be treated with respect. The villagers began to help him in his attempts to see that the maimed bodies of the drowned were put into coffins and reverently buried in the churchyard.

The problem of the many poor in the parish however remained, and their plight lay heavily on Hawker's conscience. There was little he could do to improve conditions generally but he assisted whenever he could. He upheld the cause of the labourers and his generosity knew no bounds. The very idea that others were in need impelled him to seek them out at all times to relieve their suffering.

His intense sympathy with the poor inspired him (as a poet who had won several poetry prizes at Oxford) to write a ballad, which began with these words:

The poor have hands and feet and eyes
Flesh and a feeling mind.

On cold winter nights if the frost was keen, he would recall that certain people in his parish had only one blanket on their beds and that they had gone to chill, damp attics in which they slept, often without food because they were unable to afford it. One of his friends reported that on these occasions, the vicar 'would stamp about the house, collecting warm clothing and blankets, bottles of wine and any food he could find in the larder'. Then, laden with these supplies and attended by a servant, he would go forth rather like good King Wenceslas and 'knock up the cottagers that he might put extra blankets on their beds or cheer them with wine and cold pie'. We are also told that stamping about his study, he would say with energy: 'They are crushed down, my poor people, ground down with poverty, with a wretched wage, till they are degraded in mind and body. If I eat and drink and see my poor hunger and thirst, I am not a minister of Christ.'

As the Vicar of Morwenstow, he himself received £365 a year, which in those days was a fairly modest income. However, he was content and wrote over the porch of his vicarage words which can still be seen:

A house, a glebe, a pound a day
A pleasant place to watch and play
Be true to Church; be kind to poor
O minister, for evermore.

He was ready to give away everything he had and at times, he himself was in difficult circumstances because he gave so much to the needy.

Mr Hawker's kindness and hospitality extended not only to humans but also to animals. It is said that ten cats were given a home in the vicarage and used to accompany him to church each day. One however, having caught, killed and eaten a mouse on a Sunday, was excommunicated and from that day, was not allowed in church again. Once, a dog strayed into the church and sat on the steps of the altar. Someone asked him, after the service, why he did not turn the dog out of the church. 'Turn the dog out of the ark!' Mr Hawker exclaimed. 'All animals clean and unclean should find there a refuge.'

His favourite pet was a pig called Gyp, which was well cared for, washed and combed. It ran beside him on his walks and when he visited his parishioners. It was intelligent and obedient and if the Vicar saw that those whom he visited were annoyed by the presence of a pig, he would order it out and the black creature would slink out of the door with its tail out of curl. Mr Hawker once commented that the pig was better behaved and certainly more disciplined than most of his parishioners. Like St Francis, the Vicar of Morwenstow believed that human beings could learn much, especially about obedience, from the animal world.

Thought

That people can learn from animals is not a new idea. The prophet Isaiah wrote: 'The ox knows its owner, and the ass its master's crib; but Israel does not know, my people does not understand.' (Isaiah 1:3)

These words have inspired many artists, particularly in the Middle Ages, to paint pictures of Christ's nativity which included an ox and an ass in an attitude of worship. Through this, they signified that the animals were more sensitive than human beings to the supernatural or to divine intervention in human affairs.

What lessons might we learn from our pets or from the animal world in general?

Prayer

We pray today for all those involved in animal welfare, for the RSPCA, for veterinary surgeons and nurses, farmers, pet owners and all who work or care for God's creatures, great and small. Amen.

Praise God from whom all blessings flow,
Praise him all creatures here below.

The Vicar of Morwenstow III

Parson Hawker, as he was known to his parishioners, not only taught them to place great value on human life and did as much as he could to relieve their poverty but he also instructed them to recognize and firmly resist evil. He himself had a remarkable instant awareness of both good and evil. This ability is a gift often possessed by those who live close to God and close to nature. Mr Hawker, however, claimed that he not only 'sensed evil' but 'smelt it'. No baby remained unbaptized in his parish, for it is said that if Parson Hawker passed a cottage where there was an unbaptized child, he would cry out in a loud voice, 'I smell brimstone.' Within hours, the child's parents would be at the vicarage making arrangements for the baptism.

The Vicar was equally quick to recognize people and places he believed to be under God's special protection. The church at Morwenstow was one such place because, he claimed, it was built upon holy ground marked out by St Morwenna herself. He once preached a sermon in which he developed this theory with true Celtic imagination. He believed too that all holy places were guarded by angels, who like himself 'did battle for God'.

His concern for the children of the parish did not cease with baptism. He devoted much time and energy to their instruction and the young loved him. At a time when few of them had had the opportunity to learn to read and write, he was greatly appreciated for his story-telling. He recited tales about St Morwenna and the Cornish saints, about King Arthur and his knights (Morwenstow was not such a great distance from Tintagel, which was thought to be one of the seats of King Arthur) and above all, about the children's own guardian angels. So great was the affection borne for him by the village children that when they were ill and had to take medicine, which their mothers were unable to induce them to swallow, the Vicar was sent for; without further struggle, the little ones would meekly take any medicine administered by Hawker's hand.

This eccentric, lovable and fascinating man, although the Vicar of such a remote village in a county which in those days was almost cut off from the rest of England, had an influence which extended far beyond the River Tamar or even the shores of the United Kingdom. This was the far-reaching result of an initiative taken by Parson Hawker to show his parishioners that although they were poor, they had much for which they could be thankful. They lived in beautiful surroundings, their harvests never seemed to fail and their hedgerows abounded in berries of all kinds, which could be used in wines, jams and preserves. In 1843, Mr Hawker issued this notice to his people:

Brethren, God has been very merciful to us this year. He has filled our garners with increase and satisfied our poor with bread. Let us offer a sacrifice of thanksgiving among such as keep Holy Day. Let us gather together in the chancel of our church on the first Sunday of next month.... On the first morning of October, call to mind these words.

Thus he instituted the first ever Christian Harvest Festival.

It seemed a harmless notice, yet at that time, it resulted in an outcry. Hawker's friends accused him of reviving pagan rites. The Bishop of Exeter reprimanded him and angry letters appeared in the press but all to no avail. The Harvest Festival soon became one of the most popular occasions in the Church's year. Even those whose faith is minimal can bring themselves to take part in an act of thanksgiving for the harvest, whether in churches, chapels, schools or often these days, in public houses. Furthermore, the Harvest Thanksgiving has become the channel through which those whose needs have been satisfied can give generously both in kind and money to those who are hungry or in desperate need - a cause close to the heart of the eccentric Parson Hawker of Morwenstow.

Thought Consider the difference between 'wants' and 'needs'.

Prayer Almighty Father, Lord of heaven and earth, of your great goodness, we ask you to give and preserve to our use the kindly fruits of the earth, the treasures of mines and the harvest of the sea so that in due time we may enjoy them with thanksgiving. Amen.

ARCHBISHOP BENSON

35 A Collector of Souvenirs

[**Note** This assembly would be suitable for Harvest-time.]

Most of us bring back souvenirs from holidays or from special places which we visit. There was once a woman who was a great collector of souvenirs. She was a Christian called Egeria and she lived in the fourth century. Fortunately for us, she wrote a diary. When it was translated from the original Latin into English, there were however two words, *interna acies*, which appeared often and which gave the translators some difficulty (and I suspect that those of you who learn Latin would also find them a problem). There seemed to be no appropriate English phrase to convey their precise meaning. In one version, however, there is a footnote which attempts a translation. *Interna acies*, it explains, means 'interior eyesight', but what precisely does that mean? It is only by finding out a little more about Egeria that we shall begin to understand this mysterious phrase.

Egeria was a great traveller and whenever she returned home, she brought souvenirs with her. It was often to these that she applied her *interna acies* or interior vision.

The souvenirs or keepsakes which you possess are probably very ordinary things. Maybe you have a shell or even a pebble from the seaside - and yet, ordinary though it may be, it has become a treasured possession - for when you look at it, you see not just the shell or the pebble, but the beach on which you found it, with the expanse of sea beyond. You may even hear, in your mind, the waves and the seagulls and feel the spray and the fresh summer breezes. If you have had this experience, then you are beginning to understand the meaning of *interna acies* - the inner vision, the sight which sees beyond a mere object.

Many of Egeria's travels were in the Holy Land and she brought back some quite amazing souvenirs - even a flower which she had pressed and which she claimed came from the garden of John the Baptist. Rather far-fetched, you might say, because you have always been led to believe that John the Baptist lived in the desert. However, Egeria was proud of this flower and kept it carefully because it reminded her of the preaching of John the Baptist.

Most of all however, she valued a clod of earth from Bethlehem and a phial of oil from a lamp which burned in the Holy Sepulchre. These two things were of the greatest importance to her for, when she looked at the earth and the oil, she saw the place of Christ's birth and the tomb in which he was buried and from which he rose again. With her interior eyesight, she saw not merely the places but the actions connected with those holy places – and these actions were, after all, the basis of the faith she practised.

She noted in her diary that one of her fellow pilgrims returned with a fragment of the cross of Christ and so Egeria wrote: 'With his interior eyesight, he will see the whole meaning of the cross in a fragment of wood.'

This *interna acies* is something we can apply not just to souvenirs but to many aspects of our lives. If we applied it to our studies, we would certainly work in greater depth and we would also discover that the subjects we study can never be totally isolated from one another.

We could even apply the *interna acies* to the celebration of a Harvest Festival, for the harvest produce could lead us to perceptive questions: 'Can we see the hand of a creator behind the produce?' 'In what way is seedtime and harvest a reminder of life, death and resurrection?' 'What are the responsibilities of wealth?' And by applying our *interna acies* we might even perceive some of the answers.

There were two outstanding Christians who were very skilled in the use of their 'interior eye' or *interna acies*. One was Mother Julian of Norwich, who lived in the fourteenth century. She, in a famous passage, described the truths conveyed to her by a hazel nut. 'Lying in the palm of my hand,' she wrote, 'was a hazel nut and, in it, I saw all that is made and how it lasts because God made it. In that hazel nut, I saw God, the Maker, the Lover, the Keeper.'

St Benedict described what he saw in a sunbeam by using his 'interior eye'. In it, he saw 'the whole world, which is God's creation'.

Prayer O Lord, Our God, give us, who seek you through earthly things, the knowledge of your heavenly reality.

The Christian Year

36. The Bible and the Manger I (Advent)
37. The Bible and the Manger II (Advent)
38. A Christmas Scene (Christmas)
39. The Twelfth Day of Christmas (Epiphany)
40. A Tourist in Heaven (Lent)
41. Holy Week (Lent)
42a. Christ Amongst the Cabbages (Good Friday/Easter)
42b. Christ Amongst the Cabbages (Good Friday/Easter)
43. Christ the King (Ascensiontide)
44. With Us Ever to Abide (Pentecost)
45. God in Three Persons (Trinity)
46. Guardian Angels (Michaelmas)

36 The Bible and the Manger I

[**Note** This Advent assembly is also suitable for general use.

This assembly and the following assembly may not be appropriate for use in certain schools where challenging a fundamentalist approach to scripture might cause offence to some Jews or Christians.]

Advent is the season when the Church is encouraged to 'read, mark, learn and inwardly digest' the Scriptures, but how can the books of the Bible, many of which were written so long ago and which are in places historically inaccurate and in conflict with modern scientific theories, relate to today's world? This is a question which is often asked and discussed, and rightly so. Many Christians would agree that historical inaccuracy, especially in the Old Testament, does sometimes pose problems. Ideas too about how the world was created reflect primitive beliefs which are untenable in the light of modern scientific discoveries. However, it is still possible to maintain that the Bible has much to say to us in the third millennium.

The contents of the Bible were produced over a long period of time by 'inspired' writers but this does not mean that their writings were necessarily faultless. Professor Dodd, a famous biblical scholar, once made the point that even 'the greatest genius can make mistakes'. Famous artists occasionally paint bad pictures but we can still learn from their masterpieces. Likewise, we can learn much from the spiritual insight of the biblical writers, in spite of their mistakes and limitations. If we reject the Bible because of its unscientific or primitive outlook on life, we are like those people who ignored the babe at Bethlehem because he was 'laid in a manger rude and bare'. The Bible and the manger have much in common for both 'cradle' the Word of God. Martin Luther, whom some of you have studied in your history lessons, once wrote: 'The Bible is the crib in which Christ was laid.' This statement was based on the idea expressed in St John's Gospel that Christ was himself 'The Word of God'.

The Bible contains many types of literature, but for the moment, we turn our attention to just one type, 'myth'. As students of English literature are well aware, 'myth' in the literary sense does not mean a story which is untrue but a story which expresses a truth. Jewish writers of biblical times often used myths of other Eastern civilizations to express truths about God. There are some examples of this in the early chapters of the first book in the Bible, Genesis.

These creation narratives do not have to be understood literally. In fact, we may miss the point if we try to do so, for scholars have long been telling us that the main aim of the writers was not historical but theological. In these accounts about how the world was created, Jewish writers were handling familiar themes and ideas of the ancient world. They have however changed and radically re-shaped this earlier material, almost beyond recognition, in order to express the faith of the ancient Hebrews about the relationship of God to the world and about the place of men and women in the universe. It is these theological truths which continue to be upheld by the Christian Church.

There are two distinct creation stories in the Book of Genesis. One has probably been influenced by a myth which was enacted at an ancient Babylonian New Year festival. At this, a fight was dramatized between the king and a monster named Tiamat. In the struggle, the king died and rose again and was solemnly enthroned. The spoken part of the 'myth' was recited to explain the actions of the players, and these words were thought to bring about what was being acted. For example, while the king was lying dead, a creation story was recited telling how the god Marduk conquered Tiamat, the monster, and created the world from her body. These words were thought to restore the king to life.

The writer of Genesis may well have been influenced by these impressive ceremonies, for his account bears a strong resemblance to the Babylonian drama, but throughout, the Jewish writer's faith in God remains. For him, it was not Marduk but the Almighty God, the only God, who created the world. 'In the beginning,' he says firmly, 'God created the heavens and the earth.' Thus the key point in the Jewish version of the creation story is not how the world was created but who created it. That it was God is not just a belief of ancient Israel but of third-millennium Christians, Jews and Muslims.

Thought

The Christian creeds or statements of belief firmly state that God is the creator but they make no reference to how the world was made: for example,

I believe in one God the Father Almighty,
maker of heaven and earth, and of all things visible
and invisible.

NICENE CREED

Prayer

Creator of the stars of night
Your people's everlasting light,
Jesu, Redeemer, save us all,
And hear your servants when they call. Amen.

J.M. NEALE'S TRANSLATION OF ONE OF THE EARLIEST ADVENT HYMNS – FROM THE SEVENTH CENTURY

37 The Bible and the Manger II

[**Note** This Advent assembly is also suitable for general use.

Like the previous assembly, this assembly may not be appropriate for use in certain schools where challenging a fundamentalist approach to scripture might cause offence to some Jews or Christians.]

In the creation stories, the biblical writers made use of traditions of the ancient world of the East in order to express their own distinctive Jewish faith. This is particularly noticeable in the two accounts in the Book of Genesis about the creation of human beings.

In Babylonian mythology, a human being was like a puppet completely controlled by the gods but in the biblical stories, man and woman are created as dignified beings with free will, made in the image of God and therefore able to enjoy a relationship with their creator. Although not equal to God, they are 'like God' and given a responsibility and purpose in the world 'to have dominion over all the earth'. In the creation story in the first chapter of Genesis, man and woman are created simultaneously.

In the version in the next chapter however, which demonstrates particularly God's love for his creation, man is created first. This enables the writer to show how the creation of woman was the result of God's great care and concern for human beings, for 'it was not good for man to be alone'. There is no suggestion here that woman was of less importance!

Once the man and woman had been created and given free will, difficulties began to arise. In order to explain this, the writer draws upon yet another Babylonian myth, the story of Gilgamesh, who spent his life seeking immortality. Unfortunately, just as he found the plant which contained the secret, a serpent snatched it from him. The serpent, you may remember, is also introduced into the Genesis narrative as the trouble-maker who caused the downfall of Adam and Eve.

This act of disobedience led to the whole balance of the creation being disturbed. Those perfect relationships which had existed between God and the human beings he had created, between the man and the woman themselves, between the human and the animal world, were spoiled and shattered. The man and the woman were now afraid and guilty and tried to hide from their creator. The man blamed the woman, the woman blamed the serpent, the animal world became suspicious of humans and man's work turned into toil and a burden. Through this story, the Jewish writer has described symbolically a situation which is all too familiar in this life: it is so easy to blame others and to make excuses for wrongdoings. Suspicion, guilt, anger and animosity then creep into our relationships with others and the ordered world is in chaos. However, the later teaching that all are descended from Adam and Eve and have inherited their guilt, has no place in this narrative. It does however illuminate what Christians believe is the plight of all human beings and that is that all are in need of God's saving power.

In primitive religions, 'origin' myths were often used like this to explain the mysteries of life and this is exactly what the biblical writer has done. He is employing these stories in an attempt to provide answers to some of the problems of everyday life. Why does the serpent bite? Why must men work? What is the effect of disobeying God's commandments?

For many people, it is liberating to be told that we do not have either to take these biblical accounts of the creation literally or to reject them. They are full of genuine insight into the problems of living, and unscientific and unhistorical though they may be, for Christians, they teach great and lasting truths about God and his creation. Thus, the Bible retains its authority for Christians, who can still claim that for them, it is truly the 'Word of God' and that for them, the Old Testament sets the scene for the unfolding of God's plan for the salvation of the world.

Thought

There are amongst both Christians and Jews those who take a fundamentalist approach to scripture, and who are therefore content to accept that the world was created in six days. How would you attempt to explain to someone who held this view that the authority of the Bible is not necessarily rejected by those who question the historical accuracy of the biblical account of the Creation?

Prayer

Blessed Lord, who caused all holy Scriptures to be written for our learning; help us so to hear them, to read, mark, learn and inwardly digest them that, through patience and the comfort of your holy word, we may embrace and for ever hold fast the hope of everlasting life, which you have given us in our Saviour Jesus Christ. Amen.

ASB COLLECT FOR THE 2ND SUNDAY IN ADVENT

38 A Christmas Scene

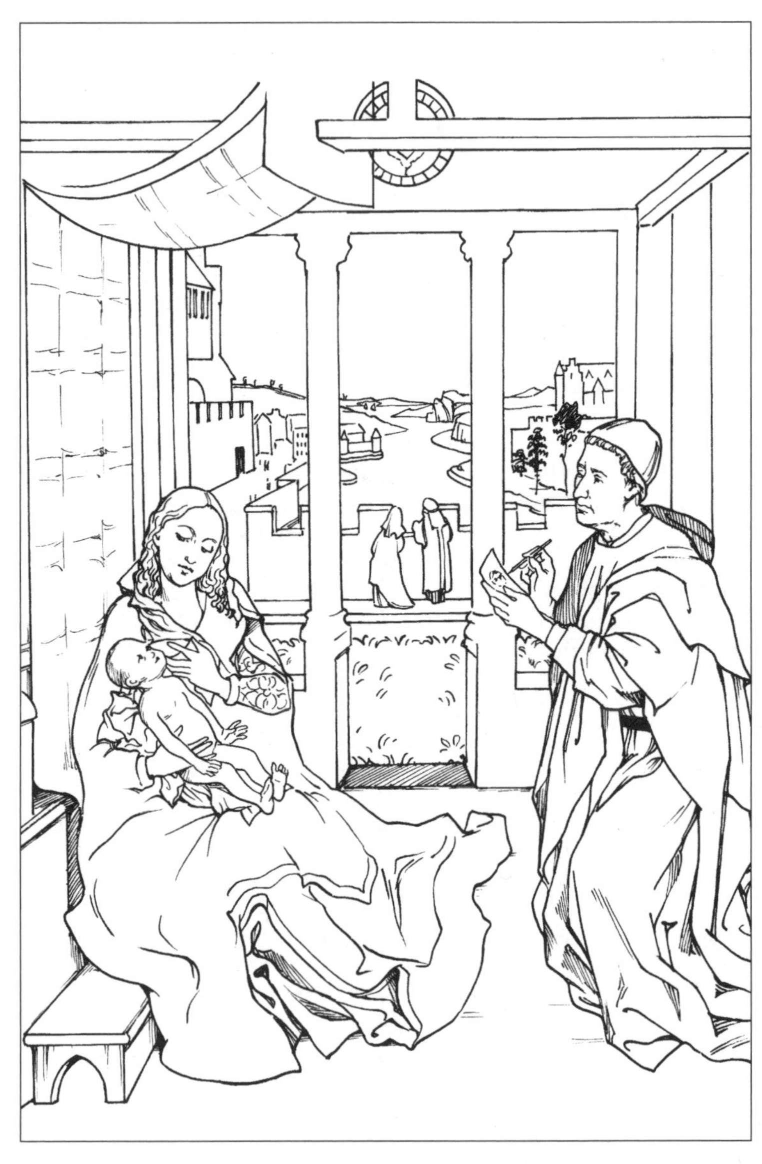

Drawing based on 'St Luke paints the Virgin Mary', reproduced in Rogier Van der Weyden by Stephan Kemperdick (Könemann, 1999).

There is, in an art gallery in the city of Bruges in Belgium, an unusual painting of a nativity scene by the fifteenth-century Flemish artist, Rogier Van der Weyden.

His picture differs from traditional nativity paintings, in that Mary's hair is not covered but hangs loosely and naturally upon her shoulders, and she is dressed in the richly coloured brocade and velvet of a wealthy merchant's wife. She nurses the child not in a stable but in what appears to be the entrance hall of a beautifully proportioned house, and she sits not on a bed of straw but enthroned under a canopy embroidered in red and gold. With her is not St Joseph but St Luke, who kneels a few feet away painting her portrait.

Beyond the carved pillars of the entrance hall and the patio which surrounds it, the artist has painted a detailed landscape. A river flows outside the house and attractive brick buildings line the banks. On the horizon, there are hills and fields. In fact, in this painting, the artist has given us a vivid picture of fifteenth-century life - the clothes people are wearing, the architecture and furniture of their houses and the street scenes outside reflect the atmosphere of a busy medieval city.

There is a tradition that St Luke, who appears in this painting, was both an artist and a scholarly historian with a great desire not only to record the life of Jesus but also to interpret its meaning. Here, in this picture, St Luke is obviously depicted as a skilful artist, for he is executing a portrait of Mary which truly reflects the appearance of the woman who sits in front of him. He was also, according to St Paul, 'a physician' or doctor and the artist has given St Luke a remarkably compassionate facial expression. He really does look as if he is a man who would have had a deep concern for the sick and suffering.

Quite apart from all these interesting artistic details, the picture is full of theological significance. Here, in this elegant house in the arms of Mary is no ordinary child but God made man. His birth is set not in the Jewish city of Jerusalem but in a Gentile town which reflects the lifestyle of a much later age. Why does the artist do this? He is doubtless attempting to explain what St Luke proclaimed in his Gospel, that Christ came to save everyone, rich and poor, Jew and Gentile of every generation - past, present and future. The Gospel which St Luke was writing also appears in the painting, on a desk behind the saint.

Outside the house, beyond the pillars, the busy world continues its ceaseless activity. Birds perch on the turret of a bridge, people walk up and down the streets, women collect water from the river and two figures stand immediately outside the house with their backs turned on the portrait painter. They show no interest in the child and his mother. Leaning over the wall of the bridge, the couple look down on the river and the man points at two ships on the horizon. Perhaps he and his wife are waiting for news of distant relatives or wondering what treasures the ships are bringing from foreign parts. Everyone in that city, except St Luke, seems unaware of what has happened in their midst, a birth which would change the world. Had the couple on the bridge looked up instead of down, they would have seen a vision of angels in the distant sky but wrapt up in their own concerns, they place their hopes in material things. Only St Luke is aware and therefore anxious to record that within the house, the most important event in history has taken place.

You will have noticed that the details in this painting certainly do not follow very closely the biblical accounts of Jesus' birth. For the artist, it is the meaning of the event which is all important - in the words of the late Cardinal Hume: 'the great and awesome God become man'. Van der Weyden is not content with the theological truths he has already expressed through the scene inside the house. He also demonstrates with his artistic talent through the detail in the landscape outside, the implications of God becoming man. Living the life of an ordinary man, Jesus had to endure and accept rejection. People, even his own people the Jews, like the couple in the painting, turned their backs on him. They were unwilling to accept that he was the Jewish Messiah and the Son of God.

Both St Luke in his Gospel and Van der Weyden in his painting show that they were well aware that rejection, although difficult for us to understand, was part of God's plan. Without the cross, there would have been no resurrection.

In this beautiful picture therefore, the artist has attempted to explain the true meaning of Christmas or the mystery of the Incarnation. He sees the Christ-child through the eyes of St Luke, who with great compassion for all sorts and conditions of men, wrote his Gospel to show that the child to whom Mary gave birth was indeed 'the Saviour, who is Christ the Lord' and 'of whose kingdom, there would be no end'.

Prayer

By the mystery of thy Holy Incarnation,
By thy Holy Nativity ...
Good Lord, deliver us.

FROM THE LITANY IN THE BOOK OF COMMON PRAYER

Thought

He was in the world and the world was made through him, yet the world knew him not.

JOHN 1:10

Van der Weyden, the artist, illustrates this verse from St John's Gospel by the two figures on the bridge. What would be a meaningful way of illustrating it in the twenty-first century?

The Twelfth Day of Christmas

'On the Twelfth Day of Christmas, my true love sent to me ... twelve drummers drumming ...' but there is more to commemorate on the twelfth day of Christmas - sensational though the arrival of 'twelve drummers drumming' might have been. January 6th is also the Feast of the Epiphany, that is, the occasion when the Church remembers the showing forth of the Christ-child to the Gentiles or non-Jews. In some countries, this celebration is regarded as more important than that of Christmas Day. Its origins can be traced to a verse in St Matthew's Gospel (2:1): 'When Jesus was born in Bethlehem of Judaea in the days of Herod, the King, there came wise men from the East....'

The first part of this sentence, that Jesus was born in Bethlehem in the days of King Herod, is a clear statement of fact and we have no reason to doubt it. There is certainly no lack of evidence for the existence of King Herod and we know from historical records that in about 33 A.D. - roughly at the time that Jesus was crucified - there were disturbances in Palestine connected with 'one who was a Jew called Christus'. This is strong evidence that Jesus too was an historical figure. It is, however, with the words, 'there came wise men from the East' that our difficulties begin. We do not know the country of origin of these 'wise men', for 'the East' could be anywhere beyond the River Jordan. The biblical text does not even tell us how many wise men there were. Yet this part of the nativity story has caught people's imagination through the ages. It has been embellished so that the wise men have turned into kings and their number has been fixed at three. They have even been given names, with which you may be familiar as a result of singing the carol 'We Three Kings of Orient Are', and they have been described as Gentiles, not Jews.

The story of the wise men, although no one can prove that it is historical, has been used over the years to express what people believed about the person of Jesus. In early Christian art and literature, the wise men become kings because the Christian Church believed that Jesus was the King of Kings, who was to be worshipped and who was the source of authority of all earthly kings. Yet, as kings, the wise men remain wise, for it was as a result of their search for truth that they were led to the source of all wisdom. From the beginning, Christianity proved to be not only a religion which could be accepted by people like the shepherds with a simple faith but also one which appealed to philosophers and scholars. Thus it could be defended by the sharpest intellects of the ancient, medieval and modern world. Intellectuals found satisfaction in the doctrines of the Christian creeds, just as the wise men were satisfied and brought their search to an end when they found the Christ-child.

The reason why their number was restricted to three was presumably because of their three symbolic gifts. Gold was a sign of kingship, frankincense of divinity and myrrh, a symbol of suffering. Thus, even these proclaimed the belief that Christ was a king, who was God, yet a man, who like all men would suffer and whose divine nature would be made known through that suffering.

The reference in the story to the eastern origin of the wise men must not pass unnoticed for that was the territory of the Gentiles, thus implying that Jesus' birth was of universal significance. It affected not just the course of Jewish history but that of the whole world.

For two thousand years, theologians and scholars have attempted to write commentaries and books about the nature of the person Christ and the significance of his birth. None of them, however, has managed to do this as simply and as effectively as the writer of St Matthew's Gospel has done in twelve simple verses in which he described that purposeful journey of a group of wise men.

Through them, he has proclaimed Christ as the source of all wisdom and authority, as God and yet man, as King of Kings and Lord of all. Having made these points, the writer concluded his story as simply as he began: 'Being warned in a dream not to return to Herod, they departed to their own country by another way.'

With the mention of Herod, we revert to historical fact and the wise men disappear from St Matthew's Gospel, having served a useful purpose.

Prayer

Give us, O God, clearness of vision so that we, like the wise men, may be led to the truth revealed in your Son and that the brightness of his presence may shine in our hearts through Jesus Christ our Lord. Amen.

40 A Tourist in Heaven

[**Note** This assembly is suitable for Lent.]

I once read an account of a man's dream. (As I do not know where I found this description, I cannot acknowledge the source.)

The man dreamt that he was a tourist in heaven and that he visited the museum of that holy city. There, he saw no exhibits to remind him of Alexander the Great, Julius Caesar, Boadicea or Napoleon nor of any other really famous men and women. He saw no pope's ring, no bishop's mitre, not even the ink-pot which Martin Luther was supposed to have thrown at the devil. There were no 'minutes' recording the meetings of significant church councils, records of important conferences or even references to Vatican II or the General Synod of the Church of England. He looked in vain too for architects' plans of great cathedrals and abbeys; nor could he find copies of influential documents like 'Magna Carta' or 'The Bill of Rights'.

Instead, in that museum, he saw in one case a small coin - a coin which a widow had put into a collection bowl and which was really more than she could afford. In another case, he saw a manger and some hairs from the donkey which Christ had ridden into Jerusalem a few days before his crucifixion. In a further display cabinet, there were three nails, a hammer, a sponge dipped in vinegar and some thorns.

The man then passed through an open door into a larger room and there, he saw an oar, once used by St Peter, and a fishing-net owned by James and John. Another case displayed part of a soldier's cloak which St Martin had given to a beggar and next to it, the knotted brown girdle of St Francis of Assisi. Other cases contained nineteenth-century treasures, the wick of the lamp of Florence Nightingale and a photograph of a ragged boy taken by Dr Barnardo.

In the last room were some twentieth-century exhibits such as the draft of a speech by Martin Luther King about another dream, but certain display cases in this room were still empty, although clearly labelled.

It was obvious that the exhibits had not yet arrived. One label read 'The head-dress worn by Mother Teresa' and another 'A bandage from the first-aid kit of a relief worker in Ethiopia'. In that Museum of Heaven, in a special cubicle, pride of place was given to one empty case, unlocked and wide open.

'But what should be in the case?' whispered the man to the attendant.

'This case,' he replied, 'is for the towel and basin used by Jesus when he washed the disciples' feet.'

'But where is that towel and where is the basin?' asked the man.

'They are never here,' said the attendant, 'you see, they are in constant use.'

There the man's dream ended, although its message remained with him for the rest of his life.

Thought What exhibits from the twenty-first century would you add? What do you think was the message of the dream?

Prayer This could be used as a Lenten prayer:

O Lord, help us to be masters of ourselves, that we may be servants of others. Amen.

PRAYER OF SIR ALEXANDER PATERSON

41 Holy Week

There are in life at least two things which you cannot control - the date of your birth and the date of your death.

I clearly remember a friend who was looking forward to the birth of her first child expressing the wish that the baby would be born on Christmas Day - but of course he wasn't - he arrived a week later.

Similarly, a friend of ours who knew that he was dying, though he had no fear of death, said when we visited him, 'How appropriate it would be if I could die on Easter Sunday,' but then he added, 'That could be inconvenient for everyone else; perhaps the day before, Holy Saturday, would be even better.' He was fortunate - he did die on the day before Easter, the day of his choice - but we cannot all expect such things to work out in the way we had hoped.

That we are unable to choose the date of our birth or our death is a constant reminder of the fact that we are not in complete control of our lives, even if we like to think that we are. People with no faith in God might well say that our lives are controlled by fate or by the stars, and some may read the appropriate columns in magazines or newspapers in the hope of finding out what might happen to them.

Those, however, who do believe in God (and I do not only mean Christians) will say that our lives are in the hands of God or divine providence.

For Christians, Easter is of great importance, for each Easter serves as a reminder that God is in control and those who really believe and trust in him will want to be subject to his will, not just at the moment of death but all through their earthly pilgrimage and beyond. Christians have also discovered that it is only when God is in control that their lives will begin to make sense and that they will find satisfaction and contentment for, as the poet Dante realized: 'In his will is our peace.'

The problem is that we are self-willed and not always prepared to allow God to be in control. We do not allow him 'to take us over'. Then things go wrong, we become self-centred (instead of God-centred) and self-centredness spoils our relationship with other people as well as cutting us off from God. It is when this happens that, unlike the friend I mentioned earlier, we begin to fear death.

When Jesus was tempted in the Garden of Gethsemane just before his arrest, he realized how vital it was that God, the Father, should have control over his life, especially at that final stage. 'Not my will but thine be done,' Jesus prayed, and as he died on the cross, he let God take him over - completely. 'Into your hands, I commend my spirit' were the last words he uttered.

God was in control and, as a result, through his death on the cross, Jesus gained life - eternal life, not just for himself but also for all human beings.

So the message of Easter is that God, if people will allow him to be, is in control from the moment of birth until the moment of death and beyond death, which is, after all, only an horizon beyond which, in *this* life, we cannot see.

Prayer

O Saviour of the world who by your cross and passion has redeemed us, save us and help us, we humbly beseech you, O Lord. Amen.

42a Christ Amongst the Cabbages

[**Note** This assembly is suitable for Holy Week and Easter.]

There is in the cathedral in the city of Truro, a side chapel dedicated to 'Christ, the Worker'. The picture painted on the reredos - that is, the screen covering the wall behind the altar - is the work of a Cornish vicar's wife, Annie Walke. She was closely associated with an early-twentieth-century group of painters who, attracted by the quality of light in the area, settled in the far west of Cornwall, in and around the fishing village of Newlyn. Consequently, they have become known as the 'Newlyn' school of artists and some of the most famous were Stanhope and Elizabeth Forbes, Norman and Alathea Garstin, Ernest and Dod Procter and Harold Harvey. Their paintings reflected ordinary, everyday scenes in the lives of the villagers amongst whom the artists worked - the fishermen and their families, the country folk - as well as the interiors of their cottages and their gardens. The pictures are now widely reproduced on greetings cards and the originals are worth a fortune.

Annie Walke's painting in the Cathedral brings together in one picture the main Cornish industries of the period in which she lived. White china-clay waste-tips and the tall chimneys of tin-mines set against a grey sky form the background to the painted reredos. Fishing-boats nestle within the rough granite walls of a typically Cornish harbour and a road leads from the harbour to a cluster of small slated cottages. There is a stone wall on one side of the road and a hedge full of colourful wild flowers on the other. In the foreground, is a field where several labourers, both men and women, are planting cabbages. A group of miners with pickaxes over their shoulders tread wearily along the road beyond the hedge, followed by some china-clay workers with chalky white hair as a result of their day's labour in the clay pits. Two women in black dresses and starched aprons lean over the granite wall gazing out to sea, awaiting the return of their fishermen husbands.

One woman with a basket of laundry under her arm stands alone on her doorstep. Her eyes are riveted upon a huge cross, which stands right in the middle of the cabbage field. On the cross is the figure of Jesus, not hanging helplessly but with arms outstretched to bless. It is Jesus both crucified and risen. The expression on the face of the washerwoman who sees this unusual and unexpected sight is one of great joy and tranquillity. It is as if she alone is prepared to stop what she is doing, to look and to ponder upon the significance of that cross, attempting to understand its meaning. The rest of the inhabitants are too busy, too occupied to notice and to allow this miraculous sight to affect their lives.

Every year, like the people in that painting, those who have some awareness - no matter how vague - of the happenings of Good Friday and Easter Sunday are faced with a choice. They can, like the workers in and around the cabbage field, turn their backs and ignore those miraculous events, or, like the washerwoman, they can stop and ponder upon their meaning and allow the crucified and risen Christ to transform their lives.

Thought

'Is it nothing to you, all you that pass by?' For many people, Holy Week and Easter are 'as nothing'. For others, the events commemorated on these days display the power, the wisdom, the love and the glory of God himself.

Prayer

By your agony and trial;
By your cross and passion;
By your precious death and burial
By your mighty resurrection
Good Lord, deliver us.

FROM THE LITANY, ASB

42b Christ Amongst the Cabbages: A Theological Postscript

[**Note** This assembly is suitable for Easter.]

How can the crucifixion and resurrection of Christ, which happened so long ago, change lives? One way of explaining it must begin, not with the crucifixion but with the baptism of Christ in the River Jordan. This must be seen as the prelude to his death.

Jesus was as determined to be baptized (persuading John the Baptist to carry out his request) as he was determined to face up to his death. But why? It was because through his baptism, although he himself was sinless, he was able to identify with sinful men and women. Christians believe that he took upon himself, at this moment, the sins of the world. At his crucifixion, therefore, Christ endured the punishment for those sins or the wrongdoings of those he came to save, giving them the opportunity to experience forgiveness and a new relationship with God. Thus, forgiveness is the theme of Christ's life and forgiveness is the theme of Christ's death.

Conversely, when 'would be' Christians are baptized, just as Christ identified himself with sinful men and women, so newly converted Christians are identified with the crucified and risen Christ, allowing him to transform their lives. In the early Church and in the Church today, the evening before Easter Day was and is a special time for baptisms. It is always an impressive ceremony, which on this occasion begins in darkness and ends in a blaze of light, symbolizing that the newly baptized have passed from 'darkness into light and from death into life - eternal life.'

In a letter to the Christians in Rome, St Paul explains the link between baptism and the crucifixion of Jesus in two brief sentences:

> *Do you not know that all of us who have been baptized into Christ Jesus were baptized into his death? We were buried therefore with him by baptism into death; so that as Christ was raised from the dead by the glory of the Father, we too might walk in newness of life.*
>
> (ROMANS 6: 3-4)

In the light of these words, it is not surprising that in the early Church baptismal fonts were often made in the shape of a tomb.

Thus Christians see Christ, his cross and his resurrection as the focal point of their faith and devotion. They observe the first day of the week (Sunday), the day of Jesus' resurrection, as their holy day; and whenever they meet together for a Communion Service (Lord's Supper, Eucharist, Mass, whichever is appropriate) to share bread and wine in obedience to Jesus' command to: 'Do this in remembrance of me', they are, in St Paul's words: 'proclaiming the Lord's death until he comes'.

Furthermore, they believe that the crucifixion, although it appears as 'foolishness' to the worldly wise, is the work of God himself, which affects not just the lives of human beings but the future of the entire universe. St Paul explains this to the Colossian Church in these words:

> *For in him (Christ) all the fulness of God was pleased to dwell, and through him to reconcile all things to himself, whether on earth or heaven, making peace by the blood of the cross.*
>
> COLOSSIANS 1: 15–20

Prayer We beseech you, O God, that as by his death, your son has restored to us life and peace, grant that by his resurrection, he may raise us up with him to life eternal, through Jesus Christ our Lord. Amen.

Christ the King

These days Ascension Day passes almost unnoticed, even in some church schools and colleges. Yet observing Christmas Day (as a Christian festival) and not Ascension Day exhibits a very limited understanding of the Christian faith.

Whilst on Christmas Day Christians celebrate the Incarnation, that God became man in the person of Christ, on Ascension Day the Church remembers how Jesus returned to heaven to claim his kingship over the world he came to save. This kingship was foreseen and acknowledged by the writer of St Matthew's Gospel through his account of the wise men, who 'worshipped' the Christ-child soon after his birth.

The concept of God as King is an ancient idea with which first-century Jews were very familiar. Annually they had celebrated, in Old Testament days, an enthronement festival at which God was proclaimed as King, and even now, Jews acknowledge God's kingship when they recite the Shabbat (Sabbath) blessing every Friday evening:

Blessed are You, Lord our God, King of the Universe,
Who has made us holy and commanded us to light the
Shabbat candles.

In the early days of the Church, Christians naturally attributed to Jesus all the divine titles which in Judaism had been attributed to God. The Kingship of Christ, the theme of Ascensiontide, was greatly favoured in the first centuries of the Church's existence. A second-century martyr, St Polycarp, when he was asked at his trial to deny Christ, proclaimed: 'These eighty and six years have I served Christ the King and he has done me no harm.' In the catacombs in Rome, Christ is frequently depicted as a king, reigning in glory. It was a theme which greatly appealed to those Christians who suffered persecution because they worshipped the Heavenly King, and not the Roman Emperor. One of the oldest Christian hymns, which can be traced back to the Greek liturgy of the eighth century, begins:

O King, enthroned on high,
Thou Comforter divine ...

Crowns and symbols of kingship are still used in the regular worship of Greek and Russian Orthodox Christians.

In the Middle Ages, the Kingship of Christ was symbolized in countless works of art and in carvings of Christ reigning in glory above the vast doorways of the great medieval abbeys and cathedrals. It is a feature which has become a common sight to modern tourists, who marvel at the beauty and balance of Romanesque architecture. Throughout the ages, poets and theologians too have frequently incorporated the theme of kingship into their writings. It was particularly prominent in the thoughts of the English priest-poet George Herbert:

King of glory, King of peace,
I will love thee

and

Let all the world in every corner sing,
My God and King!

These days however, the idea that Christ is King is often overlooked for most of the Christian year. At Christmas, Christians sing,

Glory to the new-born King,

and at Ascensiontide,

The head that once was crowned with thorns
Is crowned with glory now.

Then this idea tends to be forgotten although the great and glorious feast of Christ the King, which is celebrated by the Roman Catholic Church towards the end of the Christian year, is now often acknowledged by other Christians.

Yet, the whole of Jesus' ministry was to do with kingship. His message is summarized in St Mark's Gospel (1:15) in these words: 'The time is fulfilled, and the Kingdom of God is at hand; repent, and believe in the gospel,' and practically all the parables of Jesus are concerned with the Kingdom of God.

A few days before his arrest, Jesus, like an earthly king, was anointed with precious ointment by a woman who entered the house where he was eating with friends, in Bethany. Later, according to St Matthew's Gospel, he was acclaimed while on the cross, not just by a centurion but by all those who were with him, keeping watch over him, for 'they were filled with awe, and said, "Truly this man was the

Son of God!"' Thus the cross, in the words of St Anselm, 'became his throne'. Dorothy Sayers, best known as a writer of detective novels but also a religious dramatist, expressed a similar idea: 'Christ took the crown of thorns and twisted it into a crown of glory.'

Ascensiontide, therefore, reminds us that even the cross proclaimed Christ's kingship.

Thought

In the early days of television, it was considered unwise to show 'close-up' pictures of the King or Queen, lest it should result in loss of the mystique which surrounded the monarchy. The attitude to royalty is very different in today's age of 'walkabouts' and 'chat shows'. How might this affect our understanding of the concept of Christ as King?

Prayer

Glory to you, O Lord,
Glory to you, O Holy One,
Glory to you, O King. Amen.

Advent tells us Christ is near
Christmas tells us Christ is here ...

This hymn, now rarely sung, then traces the rest of the Christian year through Epiphany, Lent, Holy Week, Easter and Ascensiontide, referring to all the events in the life of Christ associated with these special seasons, until we come to the verse which states:

Then, he sent the Holy Ghost
On the Feast of Pentecost
With us ever to abide
Well may we keep Whitsuntide.

- but in the United Kingdom, we no longer keep Whitsuntide 'well'. Yet it is the third most important festival in the Christian year (Christmas and Easter are the other two). The early summer bank holiday originally followed Whit Sunday or Pentecost but it has now been replaced by the fixed secular bank holiday on the last Monday in May. Consequently, Whit Sunday, the date of which varies according to that of Easter, is often overlooked and its significance not fully appreciated. Another reason why this is so, is that all other special festivals in the first half of the Church's year are associated with Christ's earthly life, to which we, as human beings, can relate, but the Holy Spirit is more difficult to understand.

There is an analogy which was once used by a parish priest in an attempt to help his confirmation candidates prepare for the gift of the Holy Spirit, which they would receive when the Bishop confirmed them. Like all analogies, it has its limitations but it is worth repeating:

Let us imagine [the priest said] a writer who has a brilliant idea. He wishes to share it with others and so he puts it into words and publishes a book. It is displayed in shop windows and given wide publicity so that many people buy it, read it and lend copies to their friends. Through the book, the writer's idea becomes well known and its influence, which is far reaching, is certainly not limited to those who have access to the book and are able to read it for themselves. (The majority of Communists, for example, have not read the writings of Karl Marx but they have certainly been affected by them.) The influence of a book can also continue long after the death of the writer and may well be felt for hundreds or thousands of years - yet, the idea, the book and its influence are one.

Imagine now that the original idea represents God the Father and the printed book, Christ or God made man, for like the book, Jesus could be seen and touched by those amongst whom he lived. Just as with the influence of the book, however, his influence could affect those who did not come into contact with him during his earthly life, and those who lived in subsequent generations. This influence represents the Holy Spirit, who ensures that the love and power of God in Christ continues to work in the Church, in the lives of individuals and in the world at large, throughout the ages. Evidence of the Holy Spirit's activity can be seen, as St Paul reminded the Galatian Christians, in the fruits of the Spirit, which are love, joy, peace, patience, kindness, goodness, faithfulness, gentleness and self-control.

The power of the Holy Spirit within the world cannot be limited to those aware of his presence any more than the influence of a book, once it has been published, can be restricted to those who read it. The way in which the Holy Spirit works is a mystery, for as Jesus told Nicodemus, 'you do not know whence it comes or whence it goes'. The Holy Spirit can be active in the most unexpected ways and in the lives of the most unlikely people, even in those who are unaware of his presence and his power. Thus the Holy Spirit is the source of inspiration for good wherever we find it, whether in actions, words or deeds - and his power can have a far-reaching effect upon the world at large.

Thought

It [the Holy Spirit] fills the Church of God: it fills
The sinful world around.
Only in stubborn hearts and minds
No place for it is found.

Think about the meaning of these lines from a hymn by John Keble (1792–1866) often sung at Pentecost.

Prayer

Mercifully grant, O Lord, that your Holy Spirit may in all things direct and rule our hearts through Jesus Christ our Lord. Amen.

God in Three Persons

The legend about St Patrick and the shamrock leaf is well known. In order to explain the doctrine of the Holy Trinity, that there are three persons in one God - God the Father, God the Son and God the Holy Spirit - the choice of the shamrock leaf with its three parts in one is very appropriate, although it is not without its difficulties. A shamrock leaf is minute and it would be impracticable to use it as a visual aid in the presence of a large number of people (as there are, for example, in this assembly hall).

So perhaps it is not surprising that the Reverend Augustus Hare, a nineteenth-century clergyman, attempted to explain the Holy Trinity to his parishioners in another way. 'The sun', he said, 'is the most glorious object which all our eyes can see.' As a result of the solemn warnings given in August 1999, the month of the total eclipse, we now know better than to look at the sun but this does not prevent us from following Mr Hare's argument. 'The sun,' he continued, 'the ball of fire which gives us light and heat, can be compared to God the Father, from whom both God the Son and God the Holy Spirit come. The light which the ball of fire gives represents the Son of God, that is the "Light of the world", Jesus, and the heat which comes from the ball of fire and which produces the blossoms and the fruits of the earth, is like the Holy Spirit.'

Neither the Irish shamrock, nor the blazing sun, however, provides a really satisfactory explanation of the Holy Trinity because attempting to understand such a profound and mysterious doctrine is like trying 'to climb what cannot be reached and to speak what cannot be uttered'.

Nevertheless, this is no excuse for not using our minds in order to acquire at least a glimmer of understanding of the Holy Trinity. Many scholars past and present have written books about the subject but eventually, one is forced to conclude that the results of their labours have not been explanations but observations. Theologians, like scientists, come to their conclusions from what they observe or experience. Theologians, like scientists, do not assume that they have understood everything about a particular matter just because they have managed to throw some light on the subject they have studied. The more you find out in science, the more you realize there is to discover - and this is also true of Christian doctrine.

Early in the history of the Church, Christian scholars did reach some conclusions about the Holy Trinity and about the different functions of the three persons in the Godhead. These now form the basis of the Christian creeds, of statements of belief. Beyond that however, there has been one truth about which scholars throughout the ages have agreed - that it is only through worship that one can hope to gain any further enlightenment about the Holy Trinity. As long as people attempt to entrust such deep truths of the Christian religion merely to words, they place limits on God himself. By worshipping him however, they can become aware of the majesty and mystery of the Almighty God and of the Three Persons in one God and in so doing, can be led to the acknowledgement of their own unworthiness. No wonder Christians through the ages have prayed:

O Holy, Blessed and Glorious Trinity
Three Persons in one God
Have mercy upon us!

Guardian Angels

[**Note** This assembly is suitable for Michaelmas (29 September).]

I doubt very much if many of you have heard of the Italian saint St Frances of Rome – no, not St Francis of Assisi but St Frances of Rome, who was a female saint.

She lived in the fifteenth century and her seventeenth-century biographer Fulgiato, a Jesuit priest, tells us that for practically the whole of her life, she claimed to be aware of the presence of her guardian angel, who stood by her side spinning a golden thread. If ever, however, St Frances lost her powers of concentration, which in her case was a rare occurrence, the angel would stop spinning and would not start again until the Saint returned to her work. Would that each of us had such a helpful guardian angel!

Although Michaelmas Day still appears in diaries and the Church still celebrates the Feast of St Michael and All Angels, not many people, even practising Christians, take angels very seriously these days. However, there are many, even amongst agnostics and atheists, who will admit that there are some things, some forces, which cannot be accounted for in human or scientific terms.

People who believe in God, both Christians and those who are committed to one of the other great world religions, think of God as pure 'spirit'. What should seem strange, then, is not that God created angels, whom we are led to believe are purely spiritual beings, but that he created men and women, who are only partly spiritual.

Whether we believe in angels or whether we do not, does not really matter, for what is important, is that we should recognize what they symbolize or what they stand for. They symbolize those who carry out God's will and those who understand how to worship him perfectly – in spirit and in truth.

We are sometimes puzzled and amused by those medieval scholars who, we are told, used to argue about how many angels could stand on a pin. If however, angels are spiritual beings who symbolize God's presence, there would have been vast numbers of them, for God's presence is everywhere.

The angels keep their ancient places
Turn but a stone and start a wing

wrote another Francis, the poet Francis Thompson. Maybe when he wrote that, he was thinking of the ancient Irish legend which says that wherever God has been worshipped, an angel guards the spot.

So, whether you find it possible to believe in angels or whether you do not, at least keep in mind the importance of their imagery, which serves to remind us of God's ubiquitous and universal presence, of the importance of God's will and of the meaning and joy of perfect worship.

In a famous Bible passage in the Book of Isaiah, we read of angels praising God and saying,

Holy, Holy, Holy, is the Lord God of Hosts
The whole earth is full of his glory.

And in St Luke's Gospel, it was the angels who sang as they announced the birth of Christ to the shepherds:

Glory to God in the highest
and on earth peace among men of good will.

Prayer

Eternal Lord God,
who ordained and constituted the service of angels and men in a wonderful order:
grant that as your holy angels always serve you in heaven,
so by your appointment
they may help and defend us on earth;
through Jesus Christ our Lord. Amen.

COLLECT FOR MICHAELMAS

Past, Present and Future

Three Millennium Initiatives I: Open Churches

It may come as a surprise to you to learn that the composer Lord Lloyd Webber (Andrew Lloyd Webber, of 'Cats' and 'The Phantom of the Opera' fame) has, amongst other wide interests, a great love for and is extremely knowledgeable about church buildings and ecclesiastical architecture.

'My love of being able to wander in and out of beautiful churches goes back to my childhood,' he once wrote, 'and over the years, I have developed a great love of so many of them.' Even now, as an outstanding figure in the musical world, he gives some of his valuable time to chair a trust which aims to ensure that as many churches as possible are kept open on weekdays as well as on Sundays. Andrew Lloyd Webber himself founded this trust out of the frustration he felt at being locked out of the majority of the most beautiful places of worship in the land on weekdays. The trust, known as 'The Open Churches Trust', promotes and funds, thanks to Lord Lloyd Webber's generosity, the unlocking of church doors at times other than those for regular worship.

The trust aims to give everyone who wishes the opportunity to enjoy the peace and quiet which a church offers for thought and prayer. In areas where it is necessary to protect a church from vandalism, the trust gives grants to enable adequate supervision of the building. It is generally recognized by the trust that those who may not be particularly religious still welcome the chance to see and to appreciate the magnificence of the architecture of so many churches, the fascination of their history and the superb quality of their contents. There is so much to admire – the stained glass, the carvings in wood and stone and the impressive monuments, not all of course ancient, for church people continue to commission works of art to commemorate important events and the lives of special people.

The fact that the churches now unlocked by the trust have attracted so many visitors demonstrates that people do want church buildings to be more accessible. Furthermore, the demand beyond all expectations for a beautifully illustrated book, *England's Thousand Best Churches* by Simon Jenkins, has also shown that there is a tremendous interest amongst the general public (not just amongst regular worshippers) in becoming better acquainted with church buildings. People are well aware that the towers and spires which indicate the location of a church are directing them to more than a 'mere' building. They have realized that its interesting contents will provide them with much food for thought – a food of a very different kind from that found within the 'turreted' supermarkets which so often these days seem to be designed in the style of 'religious' buildings.

It is well known that most ancient parish churches in Britain were some of the first communal buildings in our towns and villages and that many of them date back to the Middle Ages or even earlier. Not only did they act as silent and enduring witnesses to the presence of God within a community and to provide those who entered them with a visible reminder of Christian beliefs, but they were also built to serve that community. It is in this second context that they must continue if they are to be preserved and meaningful to future generations.

Each place of worship reflects the history of the village or town in which it is set but even more than this, churches provide us with evidence of the history, both secular and religious, of the nation as a whole. In a very special way, we can learn from our church buildings and their contents, about the faith, the lifestyles, the hopes and fears in past ages and about the development of art and architecture throughout the last millennium and beyond, right up to the present day. If churches are open only for Sunday worship and the odd weekday service, it implies that they exist solely for the use of regular worshippers. The role of the buildings is then severely limited and the churches are not fulfilling the 'community' use for which they were intended. The Open Churches Trust therefore aims to ensure that as many people as possible may visit and benefit from these religious buildings which are an important part of our national heritage.

At the time of the Millennium celebrations, it was tempting to think only of the future but the Prince of Wales in his 'Thought for the Day' radio broadcast on 1 January 2000 reminded the nation of the value of lessons of the past: 'The dawn of a new millennium should not be an excuse for a bonfire of the past … In an age of secularism, I hope with all my heart that we will begin to rediscover a sense of the sacred.' What better way of doing this is there than by keeping our church buildings unlocked and welcoming to all who enter them?

Thought

John Betjeman, a twentieth-century poet who was also keenly interested in church architecture, wrote: 'It was through looking at churches that I came to realize why churches were built.'

What might have brought him to this conclusion?

Prayer

O God, you have chosen material things to be instruments of your divine grace. We give thanks for the many buildings which have been hallowed and set apart as a witness to your glory. Grant that we may show our reverence for your majesty by our care for our churches, so that future generations may enjoy a like inheritance through Jesus Christ our Lord. Amen.

Drawing based on 'The Ringers of Launcells' by Frederick Smallfield.

It was as a result of the inspiration of Lord Lloyd Webber (of musical fame) and The Open Churches Trust, that church bells were rung not just at the traditional time, at midnight, to usher in the third millennium but also at noon on 1 January 2000 A.D.

The idea was enthusiastically supported by the Central Council of Church Bell Ringers and much was done to encourage the training of new ringers so that as many bells as possible could be rung on this occasion. As a result, rings of bells which had not been heard for many years were brought into action. This was just one aspect of 'Celebration 2000', which was promoted by The Open Churches Trust, founded by Andrew Lloyd Webber. Tens of thousands of bells rang from the towers of churches at the start of the new millennium and the project resulted in the training of more than 2000 new bell ringers. With this tremendous boost, campanology, that is, the art of bell ringing, has an assured future in the new millennium.

There is in the Royal Cornwall Museum in Truro, a painting of bell ringers by the nineteenth-century artist Frederick Smallfield. The picture portrays six crotchety Cornishmen pulling the bell ropes in the damp, dark tower of the parish church in the village of Launcells. Empty wooden platters and tin mugs, which have been hastily thrown aside, suggest that the ringers are engaged in a long and arduous task. There is little time to spare for food or for gazing at the wonderful view of the Cornish moors, which can be seen in the painting through the window of the tower. The eyes of the ringers are riveted upon their captain, who calls the changes. Absolute concentration is apparent in the picture. Ears, hands, eyes, minds and bodies are completely given over to the task, which they are determined to fulfil. The caption attached to the work of the artist explains the reason for this special peal:

> *These are the six bell ringers at Launcells who rang the bells at the Accession of George III in 1760 and lived on to ring the peal of his Golden Jubilee in 1810. The painting shows them completing this peal.*

This team of ringers had therefore gathered together in that tower to usher in over fifty 'new' years. For half a century, they had rung the bells on Sundays, at village weddings and on other special occasions. For fifty years, they had been responsible for the muffled peals at parishioners' funerals. Looking closely at the painting, one wonders at their stamina to complete the peal in 1810. Certainly, one old man looks as if he is not going to survive the test. The picture, however, is evidence that he did, and when he died, I'm sure he died content.

St Paul, knowing that he was soon to die, said to his friends at Ephesus: 'I do not account my life of any value nor as precious to myself, if only I may accomplish my course and the ministry which I received from the Lord Jesus.'

Perhaps these elderly Cornishmen, whose ministry within the church was that of bell ringing, had a similar attitude to life.

Thought

Bell ringing requires commitment and the ability to work in co-operation with others in order to achieve the desired end. The members of the team are dependent upon each other and must work together 'as one body'.

These are qualities which are required of those who call themselves Christians and indeed by all who are committed to a religious faith.

Prayer

Grant, O Lord Jesus, that whenever the bells of your churches shall sound in the parishes of this land, they may remind those who hear them of your holy name and awaken in their hearts the desire to worship you. Amen.

[**Note** Postcards of the painting may be obtained from the Royal Cornwall Museum, River Street, Truro, Cornwall.]

49 Three Millennium Initiatives III: A Prayer for the Third Millennium

The launching of 'Celebration 2000' was seen by Lord Lloyd Webber and The Open Churches Trust as a means of introducing some spirituality into the celebration of the new millennium. It involved a simple fifteen-minute service of an ecumenical nature, which means of a kind which was acceptable to all Christians and religious groups. Churches, chapels and cathedrals all over the United Kingdom and beyond were encouraged to hold the service after the five-minute peal of bells at noon on 1 January. It was seen as an opportunity for people to give thanks for the past and to ask for a blessing on the new millennium.

The Open Churches Trust also decided that a special prayer for the third millennium should be included in the service and that it should be written by a young person. The prayer was to be selected as a result of a competition, and over five thousand secondary schools were challenged to submit a prayer suitable for the occasion. Hundreds of entries were received and after three phases of judging, the final panel was led by the Archbishop of Canterbury and the late Cardinal Hume.

The prayer considered most appropriate by the panel was submitted by Anna Crompton of Ipswich. It was launched at a press call at Lambeth Palace (the London residence of the Archbishop of Canterbury), where Anna, in the presence of some of the judges and an impressive group of religious leaders, read her 'Prayer for the Third Millennium'. It was then incorporated into the 'Celebration 2000' service and used in places of worship throughout the United Kingdom and in many other parts of the world on 1 January 2000.

Prayers, like church buildings, reflect and express the beliefs, the hopes and fears, the conflicts and challenges of the society which produces them. Anna's prayer is no exception. Listen to it and try to work out what world situations she had in mind when she wrote it.

Dear Lord our heavenly Father,
At the dawn of a new millennium,
In a world of darkness give us your light,
In lands of war and prejudice grant us peace,
In a world of despair give us hope,
In a world of sadness and tears show us your joy,
In a world of hatred show us your love,
In a world of arrogance give us humility,
In a world of disbelief give us faith.
Give us courage to face the challenges of feeding the hungry,
Clothing the naked, housing the homeless and healing the sick.

Give us the power to make a difference in your world,
And to protect your creation.
Through Jesus Christ, our Lord. Amen.

Thought

Anna's prayer, which is beautifully expressed, is not a prayer for a single moment in time but one that could be used for many years to come. Not all prayers, however, can be expressed in appropriate words and there are times when people find it impossible to do so. The late Cardinal Hume realized this and said: 'Perhaps one of the high points in prayer is when two silences meet: God's silence and our silence. No need for thoughts – and words get in the way.'

From Now to Eternity

'What then is time?' asked St Augustine. 'If no one asks me, I know what it is; but if I wish to explain it to him who asks me, I do not know.' These words capture the enigma of 'time', an enigma which we experienced as we passed in a moment of time from one millennium to the next. An article in *The Times* in January 2000 commented that the problem of time 'has flummoxed philosophers throughout the ages, mystified mathematicians and left scientists nonplussed, for we cannot touch time nor taste it, cannot see, hear or smell it, and yet we sense it around us for as long as we exist, an intangible medium in which our minds are suspended like specimens preserved in formaldehyde.'

Although not exactly 'slaves to time', in schools and colleges we are made constantly aware of it as we move frequently from one activity to another, more often than not summoned by bells. The pace of time never varies and yet, there are periods in our lives when it seems to pass too quickly and others when it passes so slowly that we speak of 'killing time'. Time too has another restriction. In real life, there are no magic carpets or 'time machines' to transport us backwards or forwards to other ages. It is useless to pine for 'the good old days' or to regret that we were born too soon. We just cannot escape the present and have to make the most of the time allotted to us and seize the opportunities it offers in the age in which we live.

'But opportunities for what?' you ask.

One possibility is the opportunity to turn 'chronos' (the Greek word for time as we normally understand it) into 'kairos' (the Greek word for 'a special time', 'the moment' or 'the moment of eternal significance'). This is exactly what Jesus did. He began his preaching mission with the proclamation: 'The time is fulfilled' and the word used for 'time' in this context in St Mark's Gospel in 'kairos' – the moment of eternal significance. Jesus then completed his message in these words: 'The kingdom of God is at hand; repent and believe in the gospel [good news]'. Those who, like the first four disciples, Simon, Andrew, James and John, responded to his call and followed him, found that their decision to do so at that significant moment in time transformed their whole outlook on life. Henceforth, their lives would be lived against the background of eternity.

We begin to understand the Christian Gospel when we realize that God in the person of Jesus entered into time and became the subject of its limitations. Yet he never lost sight of the eternal dimension of his ministry, nor did he allow his disciples to do so. Working without haste, he used time as a divine opportunity. In an extraordinarily brief period, he achieved so much. His words and deeds came sounding down the centuries, influencing many generations, establishing a new cultural climate and giving humanity a fresh outlook and different attitude to life.

Furthermore, Christians believe that through his life and ultimately, through his death and resurrection, Jesus did all that was necessary for the salvation of the world and offered human beings the chance to see their lives in the context of eternity. What leads Christians to this conclusion? It is because they believe that Jesus' action on the cross was the action through which 'kairos' burst into 'chronos' or through which a moment in time is understood to be 'the moment significant for the whole of eternity', or to express it more simply, the moment when time and eternity overlapped. So, Christians see the crucifixion and resurrection as events which affected not just those who were alive at the time but those who lived in the past, who live in the present and who will live in the future. Thus those who grasp this interpretation believe the crucifixion and resurrection to be the result of direct divine intervention, which enables them to see and live their lives in both time and eternity simultaneously.

Time not only gives us an opportunity to see life in this context, it is also one of the most valuable of human commodities – it is the greatest offering anyone can make to another person. We never grudge giving time to our friends. In fact, it is often difficult to find enough time to spend with them. Time is something which even the less well off can afford to offer to those in need or to good causes, by joining in activities sponsored for charity, or by collecting money for medical research.

If we do accept that time is a gift of God enabling us to see our lives in the context of eternity, the time factor itself becomes more flexible. It ceases to be a tyranny and we assume greater control over our lives. Consequently, some of the pressures appear less demanding because once we see our own lives against the background of eternity, we develop a more balanced view of the world as a whole. We continue to do important things responsibly but we cease to be in a perpetual state of 'busyness' because set against eternity, many of our activities seem unnecessary and pointless. We discover too that what we have chosen to do with our time, will not only be of eternal value but also that the qualities we develop in making this choice will equip us for eternity.

Although human beings have used time to structure their lives, it is still, as the article in *The Times* with which I began reminds us, 'a riddle wrapped in mystery and only through attempting to apprehend such enigmas, can we approach the profounder truths of life'.

Thought Do *you* think that the concept of 'eternity' helps to explain the enigma of 'time'?

Prayer Almighty and everlasting God, enable us to see beyond the horizons of this present world, so that with your divine guidance our hearts and minds may be firmly fixed on doing your will, and our lives lived against the background of eternity through Jesus Christ our Lord. Amen.

Attitudes and Beliefs

1. **Who Am I?**
   Psalm 8
   Isaiah 40:25–31

2. **'I Want to be Somebody'**
   Mark 4:2–20
   Luke 9:23–26
   Luke 19:11–27
   Matthew 5:13–16

3. **The Search for Happiness**
   Matthew 5:1–12

4. **A 'Rabbit Hutch' Existence**
   Luke 12:22–31

5. **Order! Order!**
   Psalm 104:1–13
   1 Thessalonians 5:12–23

6. **Pinocchio**
   Matthew 25:14–29

7. **Dialogue and Definition**
   Exodus 1, 2:1–10
   Exodus 13:17–18, 22
   Exodus 14:5–9, 19–31
   Luke 2:1–7
   1 Peter 3:13–17

8. **The Voices of the Page**
   Proverbs 16:20–23
   Psalm 119:33–40, 97–122
   2 Timothy 3:14:17

9. **Logs of Wood**
   Isaiah 5:1–7
   Luke 13:6–9
   Romans 12:4–8

10. **Controlling the Tongue**
    James 3:1–8
    Matthew 7:18–23
    Romans 3:21–28
    Romans 5:1–11

11. **Godparents**
    Jonah 2:1–10
    Acts 14:19–23
    Acts 16:4–10
    2 Corinthians 11:22–29

12. **The Train Journey**
    Luke 10:25–37

13. **Monsignor Quixote**
    Matthew 21:18–22
    Luke 14:25–33, 17:5–6
    John 20:19–29
    1 Corinthians 15:12–19

14. **To Be a Pilgrim**
    Romans 8:31–39
    Hebrews 11:1–3, 8–16

15. **A Box of Bones**
    Ezekiel 37:1–14
    Psalm 23
    Job 19:23–27
    1 Corinthians 15:12–28, 51–58

Heaven

16. **Heaven I: Like a City?**
    Revelation 21:1–4, 10–27

17. **Heaven II: A Place of Understanding?**
    1 Corinthians 13:9–13

18. Heaven III: Free from Suffering?
2 Corinthians 1:3–7
2 Timothy 2:1–12
1 Corinthians 13:1–13

19. A Ticket for Heaven I: Conditions of Entry
Matthew 20:20–28
Luke 1:46–55, 14:7–11
John 13:2–20

20. A Ticket for Heaven II: Accepting God's Terms
Matthew 22:1–14

People

21. An Architect of the People
Psalm 127
Matthew 7:24–27
Ephesians 2:19–22

22. The Saint Who Talked Too Much
Matthew 25:31–46
Matthew 26:6–13
Luke 14:12–14

23. A Good Person
Psalms 1, 15, 24:3–6
Matthew 13:44–46, 19:16–22
Luke 10:38–42

24. Sinner and Saint
Lamentations 3:22–27, 31–33
Luke 5:27–32, 15:3–7

25. Salvador Dalí I: 'The Hypercubic Body'
Mark 15:21–40
John 19:23–27

26. Salvador Dalí II: 'The Dream of Christopher Columbus'
Isaiah 40:12–17, 21–26

27. Two Strange Ladies I: Margery Kempe
Psalm 122
Psalms 51, 130
Luke 6:20–31, 7:36–50

28. Two Strange Ladies II: Christina of Markyate
John 17:11–19
Romans 12:1–2, 9–18

29. St Benedict and His Rule I: Leadership Qualities
Luke 12:32–34, 22:24–27

30. St Benedict and His Rule II: Living in Harmony
Ephesians 4:1–7, 11–16
1 Corinthians 12:4–26

31. St Benedict and His Rule III: Moderation in All Things
Ephesians 5:17–20
Philippians 4:4–9

32. The Vicar of Morwenstow I
Matthew 10:29–31, 12:9–14
Luke 12:4–7

33. The Vicar of Morwenstow II
Luke 16:19–31
Luke 18:18–30, 19:1–10
Numbers 22:21–35
Isaiah 1:3

34. The Vicar of Morwenstow III
Deuteronomy 26:1–11
Mark 4:26–29

35. A Collector of Souvenirs
Amos 7:7–9, 8:1–3
Jeremiah 1:11–16
Acts 21:7–14

The Christian Year

36. The Bible and the Manger I
Genesis 1:1–2:3
John 1:14–18

37. The Bible and the Manger II
Genesis 1:26–31, 2:4–25
Genesis 3

38. A Christmas Scene
John 1:1–18
Luke 2:1–20
Matthew 1:18–25

39. The Twelfth Day of Christmas
Matthew 2:1–12

40. A Tourist in Heaven
John13:2–17

41. Holy Week
Mark 14:32–42

42a. Christ Amongst the Cabbages
John 19:17–37

42b. Christ Amongst the Cabbages: A Theological Postscript
John 1:19–34
Romans 6:3–4, 5–11
1 Corinthians 11:18–26
Colossians 1:15–20

43. Christ, the King
Psalm 24
Psalm 74:12
Jeremiah 10:6–10
John 18:33–40
Acts 1:1–11

44. With Us Ever to Abide
John 3:1–15, 14:14–27
Acts 2:1–18

45. God in Three Persons
Revelation 4:6–11
Matthew 28:16–20

46. Guardian Angels
Isaiah 6:1–9
Matthew 13:24–30, 36–43

Past, Present and Future

47. Three Millennium Initiatives I: Open Churches
Psalm 122
Mark 11:15–19
1 Corinthians 3:10–17

48. Three Millennium Initiatives II: And Church Bells Shall Ring
1 Corinthians 12:12–31
Acts 20:22–35

49. Three Millennium Initiatives III: A Prayer for the Third Millennium
Luke 11:1–13
Luke 18:1–14

50. From Now to Eternity
Mark 1:14–20
John 10:22–29
John 17:1–5

Bibliography

Aelred of Rievaulx *Spiritual Friendship* (Introduction by Douglass Roby) Cistercian Publications, 1977

Anderson, Bernhard (ed.) *Creation in the Old Testament* SPCK Fortress Press, 1983

Baker, Derek (ed.) *Medieval Women* Blackwell, 1978

Belz, Walter *God and the Gods (Myths of the Bible)* Penguin Classics, 1960

Benedict, St *Rule of St Benedict* Broadway Press, 1952

Brendon, Piers *Hawker of Morwenstow (Portrait of a Victorian Eccentric)* Cape, 1975

British Library Board *The Benedictines in Britain* British Library, 1980

Butler Bowden, W. *The Book of Margery Kempe* (a modern version) OUP World's Classics, 1954

Carroll, Lewis *Alice in Wonderland*

Cavaliero, Glen *Charles Williams; Poet of Theology* Macmillan, 1983

Chadwick, Henry *St Augustine; Confessions* (translation and notes) OUP, 1991

Cornford, F.M. *The Republic of Plato* (translation and notes) OUP, 1941

Cusk, Rachel *The Country Life* Picador, 1997

de Waal, Esther *Seeking God* Fount Paperback, 1984

Davidson, Joan Marie Weiss *Homage to Dalí* Chartwell Books, 1980

Farmer, David Hugh *Benedict's Disciples* Fowler Wright Books, 1980

Fatula, Mary Ann *Catherine of Siena's Way* Darton, Longman & Todd, 1987

Fullerton, Lady Georgina *St Frances of Rome* Burns & Oates (no date)

Furneaux Jordan, Robert *Le Corbusier* Dent, 1972

Gardam, Jane *Bilgewater* Abacus, 1985

Greene, Graham *Monsignor Quixote* Penguin, 1983

Hadfield, Alice Mary *Charles Williams; Exploration of his Life and Works* OUP, 1983

Hill, Susan *Gentleman and Ladies* Penguin, 1980

Hume, Cardinal Basil *Searching for God* Hodder, 1977
To be a Pilgrim SPCK, 1984
The Mystery of the Incarnation Darton, Longman & Todd, 1999
In My Own Words Hodder, 1999

Huth, Angela *Wives of the Fishermen* Abacus, 1999

Jenkins, Simon *England's Thousand Best Churches* Allen Lane/Penguin, 1999

Kemperdick, Stephan *Rogier Van de Weyden* Konemann, 1999

Le Clercq, Jean *The Love of Learning and the Desire for God. A Study of Monastic Culture.* SPCK, 1974

Lewis, C.S. *The Problem of Pain* Geoffrey Bles, 1940

McCann, Justin *The Rule of St Benedict* (translation and notes) Broadway Press, 1952

Matarasso, Pauline *The Cistercian World. Monastic Writings of the Twelfth Century* Penguin, 1993

New Oxford Book of Verse 'Kingdom of God' poem by Francis Thompson OUP, 1981

Nicholls, David *Deity and Domination* Routledge, 1989

Phillips, Gordon Lewis *Flame in the Mind* Longman, 1957

Radice, Betty *Letters of Abelard and Heloise* (translation and notes) Penguin Classics, 1974

Romero, Luis *Dalí* Chartwell Books, 1975

Sanders, N.K. *The Epic of Gilgamesh* (translation and notes) Penguin Classics, 1960

Snellgrove, L.E. *The Early Modern Age* Longman, 1972

Von Balthasar, Hans Urs *Does Jesus Know Us? Do We Know Him?* Ignatius Press, 1980

Waddell, Helen *Peter Abelard* Reprint Society, 1950

Walke, Bernard *Twenty Years at St Hilary* Cornish Library, 1935

Wilkinson, John (ed.) *Egeria's Travels to the Holy Land* Aris & Phillips, 1981

Williams, Charles *The Image of the City and other essays* (selected by Anne Ridler) OUP, 1958

Index

[**Note** Numbers refer to assembly numbers, not page numbers]